T0162624

MAKE
ORE
ONEY

MAKE MORE MONEY

THE FINE ART OF ASKING... MOST DON'T

JACK WORTH MILLIGAN

OPEN BOOK EDITIONS
A Berrett-Koehler Partner

iUniverse®

MAKE MORE MONEY
THE FINE ART OF ASKING... MOST DON'T

iUniverse books may be ordered through booksellers or by contacting:

iUniverse
1663 Liberty Drive
Bloomington, IN 47403
www.iuniverse.com
1-800-Authors (1-800-288-4677)

ISBN: 978-1-4917-9745-7 (sc)
ISBN: 978-1-4917-9746-4 (hc)
ISBN: 978-1-4917-9747-1 (e)

Library of Congress Control Number: 2016908005

Print information available on the last page.

iUniverse rev. date: 05/26/2016

CONTENTS

PREFACE

The Whole Thing, Up Front and Easy

Why don't people negotiate their employment offers? The question has perplexed me throughout my forty-plus years in the human resources (HR) business. All during that time and even now, after hiring (or being involved in the hiring) of more than twenty thousand employees for some of America's largest corporations, I am still intrigued and perplexed, even occasionally surprised, by some human behavior when people receive job offers.

In an employment world filled with opportunity for positive and fruitful negotiations, most people simply accept the economics of the offers given to them. When I ask the question why, the answers frequently center around the notion of leverage—or, more correctly, around the perceived lack of leverage. Yet at the offer stage, whatever leverage there is will never be greater than at that moment, and still, most people fail to seize the opportunity to get more than their original offers. Explanations? Yes, lots of them, some having to do with gender, experience, education, skill, geography, job type and structure, union or nonunion influences, and individual differences that center around value and expectation models, which loops us back to leverage or the perceived lack of it.

I want to change all that. I want to assist anyone who will listen in becoming a confident, accomplished, and successful negotiator of the employment offer. Like many things in life, the techniques are remarkably simple and straightforward. It is part confidence, part skill, and part art, and all the parts are easily understood and applicable in almost any negotiation situation, not just employment. The fine art of asking appropriately just needs to be put into play.

I haven't invented anything. But after hiring a few thousand people, some patterns began to emerge. During most of my time in corporate America, where effective and efficient hiring processes were required, I didn't think much about those behavioral patterns. But when I started coaching professionals in career transition, those same patterns emerged again, and my purpose and point of view had changed. I was now in the business of assisting job candidates to get the very best job offers they could, and still, most people just wanted to accept the offers and get back in the game.

With further thought and analysis, this body of work in hiring people and assisting people to get hired coalesced into some common threads that I believe all of us can understand, value, and incorporate into our own negotiation styles for better results. I began analyzing and categorizing and then labeling these repetitive human behaviors that, for the most part, didn't work well for people. What emerged from this analysis was my realization that a small number of people were spontaneously and naturally able to display certain behaviors that I found appropriate, compelling, and attractive. The result forms the essence of this book. Awareness of a few simple techniques can alter the notion of leverage and elevate the fine art of salary negotiation for pretty much everyone. I will shine a light on a technique used naturally by only about 10 percent of the professional working population. I have labeled it requestive channel negotiation. You can apply the principles of requestive channel negotiation (RCN) to any aspect of your life or career, and the outcome, I promise you, will put you in a better place.

On the employment front, these simple principles will work for you, and an extra-nice by-product of this technique is that your new employer will recognize your uncommon behavioral comfort in handling your negotiations. That recognition will have immediate, tangible benefits and will likely also have added benefits throughout your career. The shelf life of these techniques is forever. RCN gets easier and more effective with practice; the more you study it and use it, the better you get. These techniques sit well with potential employers, and most aren't sure exactly why. In my own case, I just knew there were a few people I really enjoyed working with during their offer and onboarding process. I referred to those few people as the 10 percenters.

If you use the techniques I suggest here, in good faith, I will make you three promises:

First: I believe you will *maximize* your offer.

Second: You won't put your offer at *risk* by engaging in these techniques.

Third: You'll have *peace of mind*, knowing that *no one* could have negotiated a better package.

To maximize your offer means getting the most possible out of the employment offer at a specific point in time. If more is to be gotten, you will get some or all of it through RCN, and, perhaps most importantly, the impression you make through this process will be absolutely compelling on your new employer. When you engage in these techniques, all of the decision makers at your new employer will be even more convinced that you are the correct choice.

No risk means just that—no risk. There is zero downside to using RCN. I have never known of a single case where any candidate ever lost an offer because he or she engaged in requestive channel negotiation. Plenty of employment offers have been retracted by employers for lots of reasons, mainly because the employer discovered something about the candidate that they did not like, and occasionally they discover those undesirable traits through the process of negotiation. RCN is all about the fine art of asking, and when you ask a question, you get an answer. It is usually some version of yes. Occasionally it is a no, but even then your offer remains intact.

Peace of mind is what you are left with after engaging in RCN, knowing that you have maximized your offer and you have left nothing on the table. You will always benefit by the RCN process.

Most of the time, 91.276 percent of the time, you will improve your initial offer in some respect by using these techniques. (Actually, I just made up that number. It sounded precise enough. Remember—this is an experiential book. I leave the research to the researchers.) Occasionally (8.724 percent of the time), you get nothing tangible from these simple principles. It is a rare case that everything in the original offer remains unimproved after RCN, but it happens.

So even if you get nothing from trying this technique, you will still benefit; you will have the peace of mind that comes with the knowledge that no one could have negotiated a better package than you just did. You would not have known had you not asked.

I will elaborate on these promises in chapter 5.

Requestive channel negotiation quite simply is the fine art of asking. The vast majority of people do not negotiate; they simply take what is offered to them. In my research, I discovered that 75 percent of people receiving employment offers don't negotiate. Oh, they may ask some questions and clarify some issues, but they don't truly negotiate. Of the 25 percent of people who do negotiate, most do it wrong. My observations indicate that only one in ten people engage in negotiation behavior that embraces win-win tactics and leaves all parties to the process in a better place financially, emotionally, and professionally. It is these behaviors that I have labeled requestive channel negotiation. The other 15 percent of people who negotiate do it in a manner that puts their offers at risk and in certain cases can leave very bad feelings on one side of the deal or the other. That other 15 percent breaks down into two categories: the demand channel negotiators (10 percent) and the ultimatum channel negotiators (5 percent). Both, by the way, are legitimate channels of negotiation, but both have aspects of win-lose distributive tactics or zero-sum outcomes, which translates to an unnecessary high risk.

Simply speaking, most of the American labor force is in jobs that can be broken down into two kinds of compensation schemes. The first is *rated*, and the second is *ranged*. Truthfully, there are endless varieties of pay and compensation systems, some quite simple and some quite sophisticated, and there are some variable compensation schemes so complicated that only their authors understand them. So for ease of discussion, I simplify.

Rated jobs are those where a specific rate of pay is given for the performance of some duty. This is very common in factory production and maintenance positions, manual and labor positions, low-skilled and unskilled labor positions, certain teaching positions, even skilled nursing and technical positions. It matters little that a college degree is required; the principal factor is these jobs are compensated at a specific rate. Usually this is stated in hourly rates like $15.75 per hour, or $450 per week (forty hours), or annual amounts like $34,500 per year, as in some teaching positions. In these rated positions, the compensation is generally not negotiable under normal circumstances, and the techniques of RCN or any other method may be limited to certain benefits, perks, or other peripherals of the offer (see chapter 2). The techniques of requestive channel negotiation are applicable even in these very limited circumstances, but just the opportunity for them to work is limited.

Far greater negotiating success is experienced in those positions I refer to as ranged. A ranged position has some flexibility and is generally stated in terms of a salary range bracketed by a minimum, a midpoint, and a maximum of the range. In smaller, more entrepreneurial employment situations, the range may be quite informal. In larger, more sophisticated (or rigid) companies, range is well identified. The key factor of a ranged job is flexibility, implying a range of compensation to be paid for the job rather than a specific rate.

If your new job is ranged, and you are getting the offer, there is almost always some wiggle room in the offer (see chapter 8 on how offers are created), and you will start off better and remain ahead of the game by using these RCN techniques. I think you will agree that if you negotiate your salary before you start and make more money as a result, you will be better off in the long run (see the chapter 3 on the honey pot).

Here is the real truth: at the point of the offer, if you are the chosen one, the company wants you. They want you to accept, and they want you on board. They want closure! Remember—the company has been in charge of everything up to this point. The company designed the job, valued the job (decided how much to pay), and decided where and how to source candidates and when, where, and whom to interview. They decided who progressed through the interviews and who got to the short list. Then they decided how to perform the due diligence (see chapter 11 on references) and ultimately to whom the position should be offered and for how much. No matter what, at that point, I assure you the company wants closure—which means your acceptance and you on board as soon as possible.

The moment you receive the offer is the first and only moment in the entire employment process that the company is no longer in charge. The tables have turned, however temporarily, and you are the chosen one. Suddenly *you* are in charge. The company is obligated, extended, and temporarily vulnerable to negotiation. The company may not think so—they may even deny it—but they want closure badly enough to tweak their offer up … a bit, but only if you ask for it. The natural order of things will return soon enough. Employers like being in charge, and the ambiguity that comes with having an unaccepted offer is highly unsettling to managers and recruiters alike (see insider stories on Clarice Pluperfect in chapter 4, Roger Graham in chapter 5, or Richard Woofter or Sally Acree in chapter 6).

Now, with the offer in hand, is *not* the time to lack patience or resolve or courage. Patience will pay off handsomely. In all my experience working with people in transition, few things are more natural or more compelling than just accepting the employment offer, extinguishing that gnawing emptiness about being unemployed (or underemployed), and getting back to work. Resist that urge. Indicate that you have some alternatives to consider and ask for some time.

Any employer worth going to work for will give you some time—not much but some (see insider stories in chapters 4, 5, and 6). What the company wants is closure, and your request for some time to think it over, while natural and understandable, stands between them and you and closure. Usually, you can get a few days, or perhaps over the weekend at least. The important thing is to (1) mention you have some alternatives to consider and (2) request some time. These two behaviors are fundamental to the fine art of asking.

There is only one rule in RCN: *never, never, never* accept your offer when it is given. Doing so means you have just joined the world of the 75 percenters, those who don't negotiate, who don't maximize, who cave in to the urge to just get back to work under conditions that are acceptable but not maximized. Now, nothing is inherently wrong with immediate acceptance of a good and fair offer. After all, it *is* a job worth having. However, if you exercise patience at this moment, 91 percent of the time you can enrich that offer just by mentioning you have some alternatives to consider and asking for some time.

This is where the art of requestive channel negotiation takes over. After reading this book, you too will be able to maximize your next offer. You will not put your offer at risk, and you will enjoy peace of mind, knowing no one could have negotiated a better package. All you have to do is ask.

ACKNOWLEDGMENTS

Creating this book has been a labor of love covering a number of years. I don't have the Great American novel in me, I just had some things to say about salary negotiations. This work represents the sum total of my experiences working with people in transition, working with people in the organizations I have been honored to work for, and my own personal opinions about what works (and what doesn't) in the world of work. To my 9 HR mentors: Don Ramsey, Norm Claus, Walter Van Horn, Don Crean, Dick Reichman, Bruce Lee, Bill Barrett, Dave Wies, and Ira Dorf, most folks are lucky to have one or two, I was blessed with so many of such high quality and from whom I learned so much...thank you! To my friends and colleagues who have long suffered through this on-again-off-again process, thank you for caring about the finished product.

Thanks to my many candidates to whom I have implored time and again "one rule: never accept the offer when it is given." And then "play your A card and get some magic time". And then "Inject some uncertainty back onto the employer when the employer least expects it." Thanks to those who had the courage to ask "Do you have any flexibility in that offer?" Just as importantly, thanks to those who adopted the notion of patience during negotiations, not just salary negotiations but negotiations of every kind. Patience is a real virtue and exercising it requires self-control at a time when it requires real courage to do so. But, it pays off handsomely. This stuff works!

To the people close to me who have offered help, hope and encouragement, thank you. Your friendship, patience, ideas, counter-points, and ever-present inquiry about "Is your book done yet?" have kept me going on this project and resurrected it from the bone-pile many times. Finally a hearty "you're welcome" to the countless job search candidates I have worked with over the past two decades who have gone out of their way to circle back and let me know how successful these techniques have been for them in creating a "honey pot" of money for their future. Coming back to our Leathers Milligan offices and telling your stories about how it never hurts to ask is an inspiration to those in search.

To Ingrid and Joe Botero, who appreciated and supported my development of these negotiation techniques in my days at Murro Consulting, thanks. You both knew this was something special. To Mark Leathers and Dr. Jim Paisley, my partners at Leathers Milligan & Associates (LMA) a special thanks for believing in requestive channel negotiations (RCN) and adopting its use as our secret weapon of sustainable competitive advantage. To Dick Lippert, who liked LMA so much he bought the company and who wholeheartedly continued to support the fine tuning of RCN into a finished book worthy of publication. You never lost faith. Thank you Sir Richard.

Most importantly, I want to express my eternal gratitude to my bride, Trisha, who alternatively served as counselor, coach, proofreader, editor, and well-grounded, level-headed critic. Bless her heart, she never gave up and has read every word multiple times. To Trisha Milligan, because of you, we "got 'er done".

CHAPTER 1

An Overview—How to Use This Book

The employment process is complicated. Sometimes the technology is overwhelming, and there is much uncertainty and, unfortunately, very little feedback. In America, according to the Bureau of Labor Statistics, the civilian work force is somewhere near 140 million individuals, and the unemployment rate is somewhere around 5.2 percent, which adds another 7 million that would like to employed. Every one of those employed and millions of others not counted in the labor force have experienced the challenge of a job search. Some of those searches have been easy, some more difficult. This book is designed to lighten that burden, ease that path, and enrich the final outcome for all those who are searching for new employment now and in the future.

Among those currently employed, there are perhaps millions that are underemployed and are currently seeking an opportunity that is more fulfilling. This book is intended for anyone remotely interested in getting a job, because the negotiation process, which most people avoid like the plague, if done correctly can accelerate your retirement security and give you economic advantages during your employed years that you never thought possible.

Whether you are currently employed, underemployed, unemployed as part of that 140 (or so) million people who are counted, a student, or a member of the armed forces (who aren't counted), this book should help you. Even if you are a high school student looking for part-time work, this book is for you too.

Make More Money was originally focused on the end of the employment process. Salary negotiation is the final hurdle to overcome before you get the pleasure of being onboarded at your new employer, and as you just learned from the preface, most people skip the opportunity to negotiate in the heated rush to get to yes and start their new job. Wealth in the millions of dollars is left on the table each and every year as the vast majority of people who could negotiate choose not to, leaving thousands of dollars of wealth uncollected. I will make several references to this honey pot of money that most people leave on the table. Hopefully, after reading this book, you will ask (appropriately, of course) for more and put that honey pot to work for you and your family. I have expanded the original focus (salary negotiations) to include the upstream and downstream aspects of a job search, which should provide a helpful context for those in a job search.

I also want to introduce you to the notion that all jobs are temp jobs. No matter what you may have heard, there are no permanent jobs. No exceptions. It is globally, universally, and galactically true that all jobs end. As you toil away in your current job, rest assured it will end someday. As you start your new endeavor with the next employer, it too shall end. All jobs end; there is no such thing as permanent work. Appreciating this will help you understand, expect, and negotiate for the end (of that job) before you start. See chapter 17 for more on this.

My book is titled *Make More Money* for a simple reason. I want to introduce you and everyone remotely thinking about the employment process to the notion of asking appropriately for more. It won't hurt, it's nontoxic, it's easily done, and as long as you do it correctly, there is no risk, and it almost always pays off. What a concept!

To all the women out there who toil away next to men who earn more money and rise through the ranks more rapidly and just plain get more out of the employment experience, I have written chapter 14 especially for you. Once I got into the research on the why part of this sorry state of affairs, the causes began to make sense, and therein lies a contradiction; it doesn't make sense really. We human beings populating this planet are all products of our environment. Our behavior is whittled and chiseled and formed and polished and refined in the bubbling, crackling caldrons we call home. We enculturate, emulate, educate, and tolerate behavior from our boys that would be unacceptable for our girls, and the outcome of this environmental reality is inappropriate, unjust, and unfair. This little book might help fix that.

While the book is focused on the fine art of asking (appropriately) for more, negotiations do not take place without going through all the preparatory steps of getting you there. You must do the other things well to get you through the hiring process and to get the offer. So I have included chapter 10 about getting you there. This book is designed around the anatomy of an offer (chapter 5). Thankfully, there is only one rule of salary negotiation according to Jack. I will go into detail about that one rule and show you how to play your A card and get some time, which is part of what you must do to maximize your negotiation experience.

All the chapters of this book are designed to get you to that point. Nevertheless, you can pick up this book and go only to the issue of importance to you. If you go through from start to finish, you should find information helpful throughout the job search process. These techniques are usable if you are unemployed or underemployed. They work within your own company for upward mobility, and they have a shelf life of forever.

I will close the book with some suggestions that should resonate with all generations in the workforce right now (there are five of them), about the special effort required as you settle into your new environment and, to borrow a phrase from Michael Watkins's great book by the same title, *The First 90 Days* [1] at your new job are unimaginably important in creating a successful future. Beyond that, it is also important to recognize that the days of corporate entitlement are pretty much gone; your employer is *not* going to take care of you. You are a free agent, totally responsible for your own career development, and if *you* don't make it happen, it probably won't, so I have included a chapter on that subject.

I have had the rare and rewarding experience of working up close and personal with people on both sides of the employment coin. The first twenty-five years of my career were spent in corporate human resources work. The past twenty years have been spent as a career coach and outplacement specialist working closely with thousands of people in search of their next opportunity. These two unique perspectives allow me to have a special awareness of how jobs get created and how people get hired. The forces at work are occasionally in conflict, but know this: organizations don't get anything done without people, and the most important ingredient in providing a sustainable, competitive advantage is human capital, which is you. For employers, the best way to create a sustainable, competitive advantage is through hiring the right people. For employees, the best way to a better economic reward is to ask for more. Most people don't.

CHAPTER 2

There Are Only Two Kinds of Jobs out There: Rated and Ranged

According to the US Department of Labor, there are approximately 150 million people in the American civilian nonfarm, nonmilitary labor force [2]. Many of those jobs are unique, and many of those jobs are positions that are similar or identical to others around them. There are dayshift jobs and nightshift jobs and part-time and full-time jobs. There are seasonal jobs and rotational jobs and salaried jobs and hourly jobs, inside and outside jobs, and jobs that pay commission only, and some that pay commission in addition to a base rate. You get the point; there is an endless variety of jobs out there.

But when it comes to negotiating your salary, there are only two kinds of jobs out there, rated and ranged. That endless variety of jobs out there also comes with hundreds, perhaps thousands of different compensation systems; however, all of those jobs and all those pay systems can be simplified into these two easy-to-understand categories. Rated jobs have base rates that tend *not* to be negotiable. Rated jobs pay a base hourly rate. Ranged jobs have base rates that *are* generally negotiable; they pay salaries within a certain range, usually within a minimum up to a maximum and usually stated in weekly, monthly, or yearly terms. Now, rated and ranged as well as hourly and salaried are terms not to be confused with exempt and nonexempt jobs. Those latter terms are references to the Fair Labor Standards Act, which also categorizes jobs into two categories, those that get paid overtime and those that don't.

Rated jobs are those that have a specific rate, and usually these rates are fixed in the short term, and it is difficult for the individual, no matter how unique or clever, to negotiate a different rate. Rated jobs pay a certain rate, generally per hour but not always. Take the case of the grade school teacher in Apache Junction, Arizona, with an undergraduate degree and a teaching credential who is paid a starting rate of $35,600. If this teacher has a master's degree, the pay rate goes to $38,400. It is not much different for the registered nurse at the hospital, or the mechanic at the car dealership, or the clerk at Circle K, or all of the unionized jobs in America with bargaining agreements that stipulate the pay rate for that job for the duration of the contract. These are all rated jobs.

Ranged jobs are those that have some flexibility in the pay range. Sometimes the salary range is formal, with a minimum, midpoint, and maximum, and sometimes the range is very informal. Informal ranges tend to be the norm in smaller, more entrepreneurial, and less structured companies. The more formal ranges, represented by a minimum, midpoint, and maximum, tend to be found in organizations with a formal structure and generally speaking will also have forty to fifty employees or more. The larger the company, the more structure.

While rated jobs are typically hourly and typically nonexempt, they are found in offices and factories, assembly houses and call centers, retail stores, fast-food restaurants, insurance companies, governmental offices, and in employers large and small. Abundant exceptions to this scheme are evident everywhere, including the president of the United States, who is in a rated job. Yep, the chief executive of the good ole USA is paid a specified rate for the job. It is not negotiable, and it doesn't matter who gets the job; the pay rate is the same. It is a big rate with an abundance of perks, but it is a rated job nonetheless. Military personnel and government employees, both federal and state, deal with rated jobs all the time.

Skilled professionals are frequently in rated positions. Many health care professionals, security personnel, deep-sea divers, maritime workers, butchers, bakers, and candlestick makers frequently find themselves in rated positions.

Individuals hired into these positions usually (but not always) meet a specific set of qualifications, but the duties are frequently ubiquitous, homogenous, and sometimes repetitive. That is not to say they are not highly skilled, experienced, and professional in what they do; many of them are in demand on a global basis and command significant incomes. Interestingly, some very highly skilled employees with imminently transferable and in-demand capabilities are also in ranged jobs. You get the point; rated jobs, by definition, have a specific paid rate for performing those duties. Hourly compensated positions, union and nonunion alike, make it difficult to differentiate, and the culture and tradition of these jobs is that everyone else hired into these jobs started at that rate, so … take it or leave it. Frequently, the compensation progresses as either time or competency increases, but the position stays rated. Everyone is treated the same. Even if the employer wanted to reward someone with unique qualifications, the employee-relations problems would be formidable for both the company and the employee.

Depending on the employer and the economy and some good old-fashioned luck, many people work their way up through these kinds of pay schemes, live well, and prosper. If they prosper enough and work hard enough and, yes, are lucky enough, they usually find themselves presented with the opportunity to move into a ranged position.

Ranged positions are the second type of jobs out there, and you do not always have to work your way up into one of these. Most of the jobs that are exempt from the Fair Labor Standards Act fit into this category. But there is also a large contingent of salaried nonexempt jobs that have ranges. At the exempt level, these jobs generally do not receive extra compensation for overtime, and the incumbents are simply expected to get the job done—that is to say, whatever it takes to perform the duties required. Most supervisory and managerial, as well as certain administrative and executive and sales positions are in this category. As the name implies, there is a range of pay for the position, and the actual paid rate for any individual in the job varies, depending upon the knowledge, skill, and ability (negotiation ability included) of the individual.

The size of the organization has an effect on range formality but little impact on rated and ranged positions. Both small and large companies have hourly rated positions, most with zero flexibility on the starting rate for the job. Both small and large companies have salaried exempt positions, most with some flexibility built into the pay system. Where there is flexibility, there is negotiability.

Either way, it won't hurt to ask for more than you get in the initial offer. Remember one of the great things about requestive channel negotiation (RCN) is that you never put your offer at risk by asking for more. Even if you get a resounding no to your inquiry, at least you have peace of mind in the knowledge that you asked. Most people don't ask.

According to the US Department of Labor, about 13 percent of all workers in America are represented by organized labor, and that number includes all public (government) workers. On the private side, there has been a steady decline in the percentage of workers represented by unions for the last forty years. Members of labor organizations work under terms and conditions negotiated with the employer and memorialized in contracts or labor agreements. These agreements specify the rate of pay for each and every position within the bargaining unit. The employer is obligated to pay the negotiated rate, no more and no less. If you go to work in a job represented by a labor union, there won't be much room for individual negotiation. Interestingly, in some highly enlightened unionized environments, there might be some flexibility in the hiring rate of jobs that are highly skilled and where both the union and the company want to recognize individual differences, but for the most part, these jobs are rated.

In addition to the union positions in America, there are many others that pay a specific rate for a job, and there is very little that can be done to negotiate individual differences in the initial pay. All in all, according to the Department of Labor, about 40 percent of all jobs in America fit into this category that I call *rated*. That means well over half of all jobs have some flexibility, and where there is flexibility there is negotiability. That translates to eighty to ninety million employees in America enjoying some form of flexible (and negotiable) compensation system.

One of the things you want to know early in the employment process is whether there is a range or a rate for the job you are targeting. I suggest that you use RCN tactics regardless, but you will have more tangible success with the ranged jobs. In very general terms, the higher you go up the organizational ladder, the more likely you are to encounter flexible compensation schemes for the work. Companies have ranges for compensation because they know that flexibility in compensation systems is a good thing for recognizing individual differences. The ability to pay different levels of compensation allows the company to have a reward system that recognizes differences in knowledge, skill, and ability (KSAs) and, equally important, performance results. Differential rewards are highly motivational and create the framework for upward mobility. Most companies design compensation systems around some kind of pay-for-performance concept. This system is ideal for individuals who want to distinguish themselves in performance. Higher-rated performance translates directly to higher value, and higher value equals higher compensation—simple as that.

Fundamental to the success of any compensation system, regardless of company size or structure, is the notion of paying employees a competitive wage. Without boring you to death with what goes on in the deep, dark recesses of compensation departments, you should know that salaries and ranges are established in a relatively scientific manner. Fair and equitable compensation ranges are established by survey. Companies engage in compensation (and benefits) surveys, generally by industry, sometimes by benchmarked jobs, and those companies share gross data about their own pay practices while keeping individual company compensation data confidential.

For confidentiality (and legal) purposes, these survey studies are usually conducted by third-party consultants or professional associations, and the shared information is compiled and then reported back to the participants. Companies are told where their data fits within the total study to aid their internal analysis of their competitive position. From this kind of data, companies make decisions within their own compensation philosophy about how much to pay and where they want to position themselves within the pay hierarchy of their industry. Every organization has a pay philosophy. Most don't advertise it, and some can't articulate it, but it shows in the way they reward their employees, whether in a written statement or not. Some organizations choose to be high payers, and some choose to be below average. Some compensate with higher benefits while others choose to push benefits costs back upon their employees. The possibilities are endless, but in the highly competitive world of attracting and retaining human capital, the free market forces at work allow free-agent individuals to move within that market to the highest bidder.

Individual, free-agent employees have come to realize that their top three priorities are (1) themselves, (2) their families, and (3) their careers. These three priorities tend to shift positional importance throughout their careers, but those are always the top three. Employers have come to realize that also, and to remain competitive in attracting and retaining the right employees, they must pay attention to the employment market, realizing that the rule of supply and demand is a perpetual market force to be dealt with.

While the actual work of creating a competitive total rewards system is a great deal more complicated than this explanation, you get the picture. If a company wants to attract and retain talent, they must start with rates and ranges (and benefits too) that allow them to hire competitively. While you are interviewing with a company, you should find out all you can about their pay and benefits practices and how they go about rewarding their employees over time.

Exercise care during your interview process about salary and benefits practices, and I suggest that you follow the rule that you let the employer bring up compensation issues first. Nevertheless, this does not preclude you from conducting research on all sorts of social media about insider information relative to total rewards, including compensation, benefits, fairness, and equity issues, as well as company culture, management confidence, turnover, and financial success. Your research on these issues will tell you a great deal about the work-a-day culture of an organization, and a large part of your decision about joining a new company should be based upon the compatibility of your own personal values with that culture.

So why is all this important to you? Well, the most important variable in how negotiable any employer will be with you has its roots in the structure of the company's compensation system. If you have zero influence over the starting rate of your new job, then it is what it is, and you make the best of it, work hard, and future upward opportunities will come your way. However, if you are fortunate enough to get an offer for a ranged job, and you fail to use all the techniques available to you to maximize that offer, then you will leave a honey pot of money on the table. I am hopeful that after reading these pages you will seize the opportunity to put your new negotiation skills to work. All you have to do is ask.

CHAPTER

3

The Case for Asking—
in Search of the Honey Pot

Most individuals on the planet have negotiated at one time or another. They may have called it something else, and it may not have seemed stressful in the least. Actually, most of us grew up negotiating, and anyone with teenagers knows full well that most everything having to do with freedoms won and lost as a teenager have something to do with negotiations. Negotiating has a lot to do with sensitivity, intuition, and feelings. Negotiating also has a lot to do with preparation and research and dialogue. Clearly, negotiating is as much art as it is science.

Sometimes the best corporate negotiators finds it difficult to negotiate for themselves.

When negotiations focus on a small number of agenda items, the process can result in what we call distributive negotiations. A zero-sum game means that whatever you win in negotiations, someone else loses. Historically in this country, this was the case in labor negotiations. In most adversarial negotiations, battles were waged with aggressive words and strident positioning, and occasionally these debates ended in stalemates, hard feelings, strikes, and sometimes violence. Ultimately, either the company or the union or the Federal Mediation and Conciliation Service

(FMCS) found a creative way to resolve the conflict and save face for one or both parties. Usually some form of breakthrough was found allowing the parties to see their way to agreement. Surrounding all this has been our bipolar legislative process in support of or against the collective bargaining process that has created much of the labor code in America.

In spite of this, negotiating has been around for a long time and is not likely to lose any importance in the art of coming to agreement. It is used in all aspects of our lives: personal, professional, family, financial, and yes, even the spiritual side. However, negotiating your salary and benefit package is not like any other form of negotiation, and it does not have to result in a distributive, win-lose process. It is not like buying a car or a home. It is vastly different from negotiating a long-term purchase contract with a vendor. It is not comparable to what goes on at the swap mart, and it is worlds apart from the haggling in the street bazaar or merchandise mart or on the trading floor of a frenzied New York Stock Exchange.

Negotiating your own compensation is personal, confidential, uncomfortable, private, and exceedingly important. It can also be a win-win process by engaging in what Roger Fisher and William Ury explain in their seminal negotiation book, *Getting to Yes,* [#3] almost thirty years ago. The essence of win-win is that both parties to the negotiations get what they want. You want the job, and the company wants you—the perfect environment for what Fisher and Ury call integrative bargaining. The key to integrative bargaining is dialogue: the constant and free flow of information, the exchange of ideas, a candid discussion of what both parties want and need. From these conversations, all sorts of possibilities arise.

Most of what has been written by the negotiation experts deals with the strategic and tactical maneuverings between two parties and the mission-critical value of preparations for those meetings. But salary negotiation is different. It is intensely personal and consists of closely held information that we don't discuss with our neighbors and frequently not even with the children.

I sense a changing trend in the negotiating of ultra-high salary offers and predict in the next few years a slow but steady incursion of third-party negotiations for certain upper-level executives. Headhunters play a related role in certain high-level negotiations. But retained search headhunters represent the company and not the candidate. This retained relationship eludes some candidates who open up and share vulnerabilities to the recruiter in a trusted manner. They sometimes forget who the recruiter works for and who pays them. Headhunters (retained and contingent) won't bridge this gap, but that territory is fertile for third parties to coach, counsel, and even represent executives in negotiations of their compensation packages, and in the next ten years, these coaches and agents will become more commonplace at certain high levels.

Most of us, however, will be negotiating on our own. I'm really hopeful of seeing an upswing in RCN negotiators out there. Only 10 percent of the people I dealt with did it naturally, but it lends itself well to being a learned skill, and with practice, people get really good at it. If people simply adopt the old adage that it never hurts to ask, we're on the right track. The fine art of asking is what this book is all about. If a job has a salary range attached to it, there is almost always some room to negotiate the company's first offer.

Much has changed in the hiring process in the last fifty years. The technology of the employment marketplace was unimaginable when I started in the employment business. With new ways of sourcing, screening, interviewing, doing due diligence, doing preemployment testing, accommodating those with disabilities, and taking into account protections for alternative lifestyles, it's nothing like our prior century. Social legislation, the New Deal, the latter part of the Industrial Revolution, and the rise and fall of craft, trade, and industrial unions and particularly US government enforcement of employment, safety, and environmental regulations have taken up where traditional industrial unions ran out of gas. All of these influences along with exponential technological improvements (and complexities), global realities, and even the war on terror have changed the employment landscape forever.

Nevertheless, in America and throughout the world, the hiring decision is still pretty much done with one person sitting across the desk or table or golf cart convincing another person or persons that they can add value by bringing their unique set of KSAs to business challenges. Clearly, technology has changed everything. The methods of getting information back and forth have undergone quantum change. However, few employment decisions are made today without significant face time, and to be truthful, a lot of that time is spent assessing the fit as well as qualifications. Culture still matters (see chapter 13).

When an employer decides who they want and they formulate and deliver an offer of employment, they want closure. It is a common misconception among the job-seeking population that employers have an endless variety of choice and that they can march on down the road to another candidate with whom they would be equally satisfied. While the law of supply and demand is alive and well within the employment game, most organizations laboring through the selection process end up with their sights zeroed in on a singular candidate. Occasionally there is a candidate backup or two who can fill the bill, but once the corporate crosshairs become fixed on someone, and that someone doesn't work out, they have to start over. Employers hate that.

Three things are necessary to set the stage for your salary negotiations. First, you have to be the chosen one with the offer of employment. Second, it has to be a ranged job, meaning there has to be a flexible pay philosophy; it can't be a rated job. And third, you have to be sincere, willful, and motivated to work for this employer. Given these conditions, most people still don't seize the opportunity to ask for more. As I said earlier, approximately three-quarters of individuals who could negotiate don't. They simply accept the offer and thus leave a honey pot of money on the table.

Later we will discuss the details of the three legitimate channels of negotiation, but simply put, negotiation is not a comfortable option for most people. In their heated rush to extinguish the ambiguity of unemployment and the uncertainty in their lives, they accept the given offer. Patience is a pivotal virtue for negotiators, and negotiating and exercise of that virtue at the time of the employment offer has huge implications for your financial future.

Time and time again, Far Eastern cultures, particularly Japan, clash with Western deal-making impatience, and usually the Westerners wind up baffled by the protracted and culturally indirect process common to Far Eastern thinking. It is both a product of the Far Eastern mind-set and a negotiation strategy that the Japanese postpone talks of significance until the time is right. For Westerners, that usually happens just about the time to catch your flight home. Certain cultures strategically utilize the general impatience and short-term focus of Western impatience to provide leverage for their bargaining positions. The learning for us Westerners is that grace is important, patience is a virtue, and haste costs you money.

The same is true of negotiating your employment package; patience will pay off handsomely, and haste will cost you. My claim that only about a quarter of those eligible to negotiate actually do so is explained in part by the desire to just get this process over with. *Impatience is not a strategy.* This is the time to let ambiguity work for you. More important, the statement to your new employer that you are calm under fire validates their correctness in selecting you. Trust me, patience has a calculable payback.

Perhaps most important, remember that you have nothing to lose and everything to gain by engaging in RCN. I am not aware of a single case where a job candidate lost an employment offer because he or she was engaging in RCN. Many offers have been lost because the candidate was in an alternate negotiation channel, and sometimes companies withdraw offers for reasons unrelated to candidate behavior, as in changes in market conditions or the unanticipated cosmic implications of solar flares ... but not so for requestive channel. I admit it is difficult to resist the primal instinctive drive to say yes immediately to a good employment offer. Nevertheless, there is no risk to engaging in RCN and appropriately asking for more. I am interested in hearing from my readers about their experiences, so please send me an e-mail. If you exercise patience and ask for more, you will be rewarded. (See the Clarice Pluperfect story in chapter 4 and the Roger Graham story in chapter 5). It never hurts to ask.

This is not a book based on scientific inquiry and resting on empirical data. This is a book based on experiences, mostly mine, and created in the hopes that it can provide you with practical and immediately usable techniques that can put money in your pocket. I have been collecting anecdotal information throughout my career, and my experience resonates occasionally with some of the best-known gurus in the field of negotiation like [#4] Stuart Diamond, Michael Wheeler, Alan McCarthy, even Herb Cohen, all the folks at Dale Carnegie, Fisher, Ury, and Bruce Patton, and Kolb and Williams, another pair of female authors who register large on the negotiation scene like Babcock and Laschever. Nevertheless, I must leave the science part to the scholarly folks who want their research published in the *Harvard Negotiations Journal*. This work is not one of those. You are my laboratory, and your experiences matter to me, so send me an e-mail.

Most of us ordinary human beings do not normally base our buy decisions on negotiating successfully. Most of our buy decisions are at fixed prices, and the notion of fixed-price merchandizing is one of the stabilizing influences of our great society. Can you imagine the chaos if everyone negotiated everything they bought at Safeway or haggled over the cost of the movie or a gallon of gasoline?

Nevertheless, this behavior is expected in certain industries and markets. Who walks into a car dealership these days and pays sticker price? Knowing this, the whole psychology of avoiding negotiation has been the basis for more than one national chain of auto dealers who base their whole business on "the sticker price is *the* price"—no hassle, no pressure, and no commissions to the salesperson who is the most successful at sucking the most money out of your wallet.

The recognition that the sticker price is *the* price puts a whole new feel to the experience of buying a used car. The no-negotiation price strategy works well and significantly changes the structure of the deal. It works because of our natural inclination to avoid haggling whenever possible. One of the unintended consequences also resonates with the cognoscenti: it encourages the thoughtful among us to educate ourselves before we engage in the buying experience. Knowing the value of the coveted vehicle is the way we guard against being fleeced. It's the antidote to naivety.

Car dealerships know this, and they also know that it is impossible for you to research the multiple manufacturers represented on their lots, and they know that it is highly likely that you will make an emotional decision to purchase your vehicle anyway. Once loosed upon the lot, the buyer inevitably finds the make and color of their dreams based upon emotion more than upon logic and preparation. The point is it becomes much more comfortable to do the deal when you know that negotiations are not going to be part of the process. It is a much more comfortable experience, much like everything else we buy. By comparison, if we negotiated everything we purchased every time, the bartering process would become very messy indeed. Most of us accept the price as marked, and it becomes an expected part of life.

The largest purchase we usually make is the purchase of our home, and in most markets around the country—around the world actually—negotiation is the expected process. The listing realtor and the buyer, after doing their research, arrive at a listing price. This is only rarely the price the home sells for, and everyone knows it. In some rare markets where demand outstrips supply, the price may actually enjoy a bidding-up process, but that is truly the exception. The rule is usually in the other direction, and buyers almost always respond to the asking price by making an offer that is 85 to 95 percent of the asking price. A couple of gambits back and forth, and an agreement is reached ... or not.

There is a common and ordinary expectation of negotiations in most of the large purchases in our lives, certainly in cars and houses. Here's the real deal: the consequence of these negotiations measured in real dollars is totally eclipsed by the importance of negotiating your own personal compensation. Still, most people don't. Pause for a moment and think through the difference in wealth accumulation if you start 3, 5, or 10 percent higher in your base cash compensation and pyramid that higher amount over your working career. The impact is astonishing; hundreds of thousands of dollars go unclaimed every day of every year by candidates who accept what they are offered without asking for more. Most of you can't wait to accept and get started on the new job.

If we would calculate the actual impact that salary negotiations can have on our economic well-being, salary negotiations would become much more compelling than negotiating for a home or a car. We spend a lot of time and energy negotiating for a few thousand dollars on these purchases, yet without even thinking about it, we leave hundreds of thousands of dollars with the employer rather than in our pocket because we fail to negotiate. I call that leaving a honey pot of money on the table. Let's resolve not to do that.

Do the math. Set up a compounding table on an investment of (pick a number) somewhere between 3 percent and 10 percent of your compensation and calculate it out over the course of your working years. It's a big number, this honey pot—like millions of dollars over the course of a forty-year career [#5]. See the Babcock and Laschever example below, [#6] which is just as relevant today as when it was published in their book ten years ago.

Consider this example: Say a man and a woman both receive identical first-job offers at age twenty-two for $35,000. The man asks and successfully negotiates his starting salary to $36,505 (4.3 percent). The woman asks and successfully negotiates a starting salary of $35,945 (2.7 percent). Although the difference in their starting salaries of only $560 may seem small, consider what happens if this same pattern continues over the course of their career until retirement at sixty-five (his salary going up by 4.3 percent and hers going up 2.7 percent annually). By the time they retire, he is making an annual salary of $213,941, and she is earning $110,052, just about half of what his salary is. Even worse, if he invests the difference between their salaries in an account earning only 3 percent per year, he will accumulate an additional $2,120,731 in his honey pot, and that's not chump change. These calculations don't account for the woman's comparative losses in retirement and pension benefits, which are typically tied to earnings. Modest differences can add up to huge disparities over time. This honey pot thing is not trivial.

Salary negotiation is clearly different from other forms of negotiation. You could read thirty high-powered books on negotiation strategies and be left with little that is appropriate for your personal strategy for salary negotiation. If you read just three classics—*Women Don't Ask* by Babcock and [6] Laschever, *Getting to Yes* by Fisher, Ury, and Patton [3], and *Make More Money* (how self-serving) by Milligan [8]—you should have everything you will ever need to handle a lifetime of salary negotiations. This subject is intensely personal. You don't do it every day, but the mere thought of it strikes fear, trepidation, and (wait for it …) avoidance into the hearts of everyone who has ever prepared and interviewed well, received an offer, and paused at that moment of truth to consider … *dare I ask for more?* Avoidance is toxic to honey pots.

Let's put some certainty into all that. All you have to do is ask.

Seventy-Five Percent of People Who Could Negotiate Don't. Of the 25 Percent Who Do, Most Do It Wrong. Clarice Did It Right

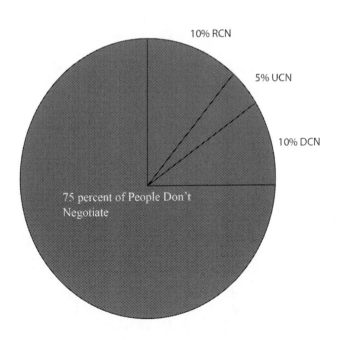

10% RCN

5% UCN

10% DCN

75 percent of People Don't Negotiate

The vast majority of people who could negotiate don't do it. They accept the offer they are given and are darned happy to get it. But they leave that honey pot full of money sitting on the table.

Make More Money is not a scientifically validated research study. I have no control groups and no randomly selected Solomon four-group design research protocols. But I have personally hired thousands of people, and I have been responsible for the hiring of thousands more through the people that reported to me. I have coached thousands of middle- and upper-level managers through career transition and assisted them in every stage of their search, including the negotiation stage. My career in human resources was split between these two opposing objectives. The first was in corporate America, where I toiled for three decades in the trenches of what is now called human resources, during which time I was involved in hiring over twenty thousand people with the objective of maximizing the talent and minimizing the expense. The second and most personally rewarding segment has been as a career coach in executive outplacement for the last twenty (or so) years. These two related but separate experiences have given me the learning laboratory to observe, develop, and test my negotiation theory with a large volume of people in talent acquisition and career transition and the negotiating processes from both perspectives.

What follows are the summary results of my categorization of those experiences. Keep in mind that my experiential frame of reference is focused mostly in financial services, fabrication and assembly centers, offices, machine shops, factories, technical service centers, computer and software design and manufacturing, call centers, and large health care environments. These observations come from thousands of iterations with people in actual employment experiences, and while I believe these experiences are transferable to employment situations everywhere, they may not be. But to the millions of potential readers who can gain from utilizing my techniques no matter what their field of endeavor, I say bravo; it never hurts to ask.

My actual experience is that fully three-quarters of those who could negotiate do not. In other words, 75 percent of those I made job offers to for ranged jobs did not engage in any form of negotiation. When questioned about this, these same individuals indicated a half-dozen themes again and again:

- The offer was fair, and they were tired of looking.
- They didn't think they had any leverage to negotiate.
- They didn't want to risk losing the job offer.
- They didn't want the company to think bad things about them.
- If they tried to negotiate, they might injure a fragile relationship with the company.
- And the feminine favorite: they wanted to get started, demonstrate their competency, and then they would be rewarded with a raise (see chapter 14 on gender differences).

From my observations about people in employment situations, when the time comes for negotiations, they tend to do so (or not do so) within the parameters of their personal style, their confidence, and their assessment of their situational risk. Of the 25 percent of candidates who do negotiate, I have observed and categorized three legitimate styles or "channels" of negotiations they use. They are as follows:

- ultimatum channel negotiation (UCN)
- demand channel negotiation (DCN)
- requestive channel negotiation (RCN)

All three are legitimate negotiation channels to use, depending upon an individual's style and circumstances. All involve some form of dialogue, some back and forth iterative process that we fairly label as negotiation. All have different success rates. Interestingly, only requestive channel negotiation (RCN) has a consistently positive outcome for all parties.

Which one you choose makes a vastly different statement to the prospective employer. Each has its place, and each is appropriate in certain circumstances. Requestive channel negotiation is my personal favorite because it makes a far better impression on the organization, makes a considerably more positive statement about the candidate, establishes a win-win flavor to the process, and tends to provide tangible results approximately nine out of ten times.

These three styles, or channels as I call them, are generally representative of the behavior that I have observed people adopt in their response to an employment offer. Interestingly, these behaviors are predictable based upon behavioral characteristics demonstrated during the recruiting process. Astute talent-acquisition professionals should be able to accurately predict these reactive behaviors before the offer is extended.

An analysis of the behavior of thousands of people at the acceptance stage indicates one additional channel of communication that people engage in, called Probative Channel. The three legitimate negotiation channels you have heard about so far (UCN, DCN, and RCN) are actual negotiation strategies. For clarification purposes, probative channel communication is *not* one of these; it is used to get clarity and detailed understanding of a benefit, policy, or cultural question. Most prospective employees, at or before the offer, ask questions about their new company. Many probative questions demonstrate the candidate has done his or her homework about the company. Probative communication should not be confused with the three negotiation channels. Probative channel is all about getting the basic questions answered before a final decision can be made. For instance, when is the first performance review? This is a legitimate question. As is, how is performance evaluated? Likewise, what is the latitude for decision making? How is conflict resolved? One of my favorites, is the cafeteria food any good? All are appropriate questions, and all are followed by a question mark at the end of the sentence. But these are clarity questions, not actual requests for more.

There are questions about the organizational culture, the salary range, bonus income potential, promotional opportunities, training expectations, vacation allowance, and on and on. Good questions all, but getting clarity about how things are done in a company is *not* the same thing as asking for more once you have received the offer. If you are reading this as a candidate, please remember that all of the clarity questions, all of the probative inquiry, must be complete *before* any negotiations can begin. You have to gain a complete and thorough understanding of the job, the boss's expectations, the company history and culture, the performance evaluation, the review and reward process, potential for upward mobility, the industry and the company's placement within that industry, and the global reality of change. While it helps to have a healthy dose of tolerance for ambiguity, I recommend that you reduce controllable uncertainty to a minimum. We do this with probative inquiry, but this is not negotiating.

Asking for more is the essence of the actual negotiation process. Probative and requestive channel do share a question mark at the end of the sentence. As you will see below, punctuation at the end of the sentence is one of the illustrative ways you can remember the differences between the three negotiation channels. Ultimatum channel tends to have an exclamation point (!) at the end of the sentence and enjoys the highest rate of failure. Demand channel tends to have a period (.) at the end of the sentence, and while it is certainly less flamboyant than ultimatum channel, it too has a high level of failure. Requestive channel negotiation is distinguished by a question mark (?) at the end of the sentence, and it never fails. It never fails as a negotiation technique because you are asking for more, and when you ask a question, you get an answer. While your answer can include a lot of information, it comes basically as a yes or a no. Even when you get a no answer, it does not threaten or alter the original offer, and it usually comes with an elaborate, almost apologetic explanation of why the answer is no.

Ultimatum Channel Negotiation

As you can tell from the pie chart, only (less than) 5 percent of candidates engage in ultimatum channel negotiations. Ultimatum channel is a highly legitimate negotiation channel, but the circumstances that make it work are the same circumstances that cause it to fail, and it fails often. The high-risk propensity of candidates and their low-risk circumstances, more than their style, are what usually encourages this negotiation tactic. Those engaging in UCN are usually currently employed and very well situated. They may be flattered by the attention and temporarily intrigued by the possibilities, but they don't have a driving *need* for a new opportunity. I encountered this type of individual mostly when reaching out either through sourcing efforts (internal or external) or pure networking or retained search. Actually, most of these situations end up on the scrap heap pretty early, and they are the bane of existence for headhunters. Sometimes the company rethinks hiring a person that engages in this channel and sometimes even rescinds the offer based on these behaviors. Sometimes the company simply abandons the negotiations. This tactic is successful only about 40 percent of the time. I use successful very reluctantly because even when it works, negative impressions linger.

Candidates engage in ultimatum tactics when they can afford to walk away from the offer. UCN either enjoys or is cursed with the highest level of failure of all three channels. Fifty to 60 percent of this category goes down in flames. Even the ones that work out usually leave a very bitter aftertaste with the recruiter and the hiring manager and perhaps even some of the team already on board. Depending upon the job, the skill of the individual, the vulnerability of the company, the timing, the market conditions, perhaps the phase of the moon, and the conditions under which ultimatum channel negotiations are conducted, someone (usually within the company) will feel used and abused. These memories tend to last.

The candidate behavior exhibited in ultimatum channel is generally take it or leave it. The company has searched, found, and wooed the individual with the express purpose of recruiting this particular talent away from wherever he or she was found. These conditions are very advantageous to the candidate, and just as in any negotiations, whenever one party has a decided advantage, the process can be pretty one-sided. Companies much more frequently than candidates tend to enjoy the advantages of upperhanded leverage and tend to drive employment cost down with that advantage whenever they can. Market factors rule.

Certain individuals who develop a truly rare skill set can find themselves in equally well-leveraged positions when companies come calling. It is those same individuals who find themselves able to put forth an ultimatum, which when compared to the demand channel is both higher in actual value and more dismissive in attitude. These candidates have the luxury of being able to drive a very hard bargain and adopt an ultimatum attitude. The company will have to pay the ransom or move on to search for another candidate. In these situations, there aren't a lot of candidates, and the company is vulnerable because of a need for scarce resources. But keep in mind, in my experience, ultimatum channel negotiations occur in something less than 5 percent of all cases.

At its core, UCN goes something like this: "I really appreciate your offer, and I am flattered that you have gone to all this work. But (pause), it's going to take $$$ to get me to leave my great job at Acme Tool Company!" The "$$$" is almost always a third to half again as much as the initial offer, sometimes even more, and it doesn't even come with an apology. The amount is excessive, and the tone borders on cocky and abrasive. The individual can afford to drive a hard bargain, and they know it. In my experience, this is almost exclusively male behavior. As you see, the punctuation (!) at the end of the sentence is an exclamation point. An exclamation point is a fitting and proper symbol to represent this style of negotiation.

As I said, over half end up on the cutting room floor, and the ones that do work their way to acceptance almost always engender hard feelings. Even when these lopsided negotiations result in an agreement, one party to the process feels the uncomfortable edge of a zero-sum game. In other words, someone has to lose big for someone else to win big. Resentment is the natural by-product of this process, and in my experience, even when they accept, they fall apart as often as they succeed. No one likes to receive an ultimatum. "Take it or leave it" puts people in a corner. Some individuals in business have long memories, and the tides of fortune always ebb and flow.

Demand Channel Negotiation

About 10 percent of individuals fall into this category, and without thinking about it, they engage in demand channel negotiation automatically. These folks gravitate naturally to demanding more.

They are like the rest of us in most outward appearances, but they know in their hearts that no matter what the company offers, there is always more there to be had. All you have to do is reach out and get it. By their very nature, the DCNs of the world understand the nature of the give-and-take process. That is exactly how they see the employment offer. They tend to be in-charge people and aggressive by nature. Driven by a need to succeed, frequently these people view the job, the title, the employment process, and the salary they make as a mantle of their success. They have a personality-driven need for success, and they are constantly in the search for something bigger and better. Some tend to disguise it better than others, but this negotiation style is a function of personality only, not personality *and* circumstance as in UCN.

For these intrepid individuals, most of whom are employed but some are in transition and in a full-time job search, getting more from the offer is a challenge, and they tend to approach it head on. Many in this category approach the process with an expectation that employers negotiate to get talent as inexpensively as possible. Many in this 10 percent category engage in DCN as an extension of their everyday life. No matter what the employer throws out there, there is always another (higher) number, and they don't mind putting it out there as a demand. It goes something like this: "Thanks for the offer of $85,000. I appreciate it, and I know I can add value to Acme Corp. I am currently making close to that amount, and I need something closer to $100,000." The punctuation at the end of the sentence is a period. There are clear differences between this and the ultimatum channel. The number demanded is higher but not outlandish (like UCN). The tone is softer and easier to take but is still a demand. Companies are as free to walk away from demands as they are from ultimatums but less inclined to do so.

The failure rate is not as high as UCNs, but it is still in the 15 percent to 20 percent category, depending upon level and market forces. The tone of the candidate is pushy perhaps aggressive. Most talent managers, recruiters, and hiring managers react more favorably to demand channel negotiators than ultimatum channel negotiators. The employer response can be either to hold tight or counter or pursue another candidate. Fortunately, most employers want closure and will stick with the demand channel candidate and either counter with something appropriate or reaffirm the original offer but remain unchanged. Sometimes other items can serve as quid pro quo for salary issues. Remember—only about 10 percent of job-seeking individuals fit into this category, and fortunately for them, most offers work out. Very few women engage in this channel, more certainly than in ultimatum channel, but in my experience, this is still 80 percent male territory.

The downside is that a certain percentage of these fail. Employers decide not to pursue it any further with this candidate for one or more of the obvious reasons. Perhaps the edge on the employee is too sharp, perhaps the demand is too high, perhaps there are interchangeable alternative candidates, perhaps the nephew of the owner needs a job. Stuff happens.

Requestive Channel Negotiation

Another 10 percent of the general population fit in here, and more than the other two categories, these people seem to do it naturally and agreeably. This percent of the population gravitates to a behavioral style that is requestive and based on positive inquiry. Like the demand channel people, these individuals engage in this channel as a function of their personality more so than circumstances. They possess many of the same traits of DCN people, but they articulate it differently. Requestive channel negotiators tend to be upwardly motivated and career-focused professionals who are by nature a little more aware of their impact on others. They are sensitive to the fragile nature of the employment offer, but they are usually win-win negotiators who engage in integrative style negotiations. Their behavior is marked by a collaborative spirit and a free flow of information. Most of these people are easier to get along with and sincerely interested in collegial respect. They are not afraid to ask for more, and that is the defining trait of this category. They tend to understand that the employment relationship is a business transaction where both parties have something the other wants. By nature, they instinctively know that there are flexible parameters to the offer, and their task is find out where that flexibility is and maximize it for their benefit.

RCNs tend to ask a lot of questions and engage in Probative Channel for clarity with an easy approach that is conversational and friendly. They tend to get the details of the employment relationship nailed down early and appropriately. Any lingering questions they may have about working for the company tend to be technical in nature and are almost always vetted before the offer stage.

Requestive channel negotiators tend to do their homework and exhibit another behavioral gem: they ask for time to consider the offer. This was one of my most interesting observations of this type. Not all but most candidates who engaged this way would ask for time to discuss the offer with their spouse/family/friend/rabbi or dog before acceptance. This put the whole employment process into a hold until they came back to me with an answer. It took me years to correlate the relationship between the probative behavior, the request for time, and the tendency to ask for more in the offer. I clearly enjoyed working with these individuals, even more than the multitudes who simply accepted the offer as presented. These individuals represented a rare challenge, all the while exhibiting complex behavior that put a new wrinkle into the recruitment process—time to consider the offer.

Most importantly, during this time, I was not in control. The candidate had us over a barrel. The company was obligated, and we had no closure with the candidate. I was obligated to wait it out. During this time ... sometimes only a day but as long as a week, depending upon the circumstances, human nature takes over, and the hiring manager and I started to fill the void with negative thoughts. More on that in chapter 8, but experiencing this reality provided me with one of the most important elements of this channel: ambiguity and uncertainty at this stage are new experiences for the company, and it does tend to position the company for negotiating in a positive way. Most candidates, and in truth most hiring managers, never acknowledge the significance that this is the only moment in the employment process that the company is *not* in charge.

Another issue occurred with this group of candidates, and the rarity of this occurrence combined with the request for time was the only reason I tied these two behavioral issues together. Occasionally, a candidate would presage his or her request for time with the notion that she had some alternatives to consider and then would request some time to consider the offer. Never a lot of time but sufficient to impress me that I was not in charge during this hiatus. These two issues combined create the two essential techniques of RCN that make it so compelling.

Now experienced talent-acquisition professionals are astute at picking up indications that might threaten their hit rate for offers made / offers accepted. This is one of the important metrics most sophisticated organizations use to measure their recruiting success. So my antenna would go up the instant I heard "alternatives," because coming from a candidate that we really wanted, alternatives that deserve to be considered generally meant the candidate had other offer(s) to consider. This notion that my candidate had alternatives *and* wanted some time to think about the offer formed the essential ingredients of RCN.

Frequently, issues around relocation further complicate the negotiations, and I have included chapter 9 to focus on relocation challenges.

Almost always, employment offers are made over the telephone. Clearly, some are sent by e-mail and by letter, and some are made in person, but most tend to be delivered by phone after the company has finished its selection process and worked out the highly sophisticated and little understood voodoo art of creating the terms of the employment offer (see chapter 8). As in the case of Clarice Pluperfect, it went something like this: "Hello, Clarice. This is Jackson Staffermogul from Acme Corporation. Do you have a few minutes to talk? Okay good! On behalf of Chris Newboss with whom you have interviewed and will report to, it is our pleasure to extend you a contingent offer of employment." Then would come the details of the written offer and the contingencies (usually drug testing), followed by an indication that I was sending the offer to her home by e-mail or Fed Ex. Then I would generally follow up with, "Well, what do you think?" Most responses were immediate and enthusiastic; this let me know I had made the offer to someone genuinely excited to receive it. It is important in multiple ways for recruiters to obtain acceptance and start dates during that call. An experienced recruiter gets a feel for the candidate right away in this conversation and can usually predict the outcome from the sound bites the candidate gives during the first few minutes of the conversation. But for these ten percenters, after the validating and enthusiastic response would come the inevitable words "So I'm really excited about the opportunity, but now I have some alternatives to consider, and ... well, this is an important decision for me and my family, and I would appreciate some time to think about it. Could I have till next Whateverday to think it over?"

Now there is a little-known but high-intensity job requirement for recruiters that acceptance and start date is to be immediately conveyed back to the hiring manager, who is anxiously awaiting this confirmation, immediately after the offer call. In the case of these 10 percenters, that was not in the cards. In fact, my call to Chris Newboss was downright unsettling. This double-whammy experience of not having an acceptance or a start date *and* suspecting our candidate had some alternative offers in the mill was something that I and all recruiters dreaded.

Being the reputable firm that we were and agreeing that it indeed was an important decision, I would give her the requested time. Meanwhile, back at Chris Newboss's office, things were coming unhinged. Chris really wanted/needed Clarice to join the team, and the mere thought that she might not had not occurred to Chris. She called me and only modestly covered her panic and inquired what could she possibly need time to consider the offer for. After all, she had interviewed with everyone on the team and with Chris at least two times ... and then nonstop she inquired if there were any unanswered questions on issues she had discussed. I assured her there were none. Then more nonstop speculation that maybe Clarice had informed her employer she was coming to us, and they immediately countered ... Or perhaps she had another offer in or coming in, and she wanted some time to consider the alternative ... and then more nonstop to revisit what salary we had offered her. Was it enough? ... And finally Chris Newboss, now completely unhinged, suggested to me that we call Clarice back and sweeten the offer by another significant amount. Chris was in rare form, and it took every skill set I had to convince her to let the situation work itself out. She was not a happy supervisor and was very worried that her prize new recruit was opting out. All of this drama, all of this uncertainty and worry because of two simple sentences: "I have some alternatives I need to consider" and "May I have some time to think it over?"

Eventually, when Clarice called me back, she immediately revalidated her interest in the job. At that instant, a fly on the wall in my office would have observed a visible/audible sigh of relief as the expectation of the worst faded away. Clarice was going to accept but had a couple of questions about her offer. Somehow as if by magic, Chris showed up at my office door, clearly and visibly on edge about what Clarice was saying.

After Clarice had shared her enthusiasm for working at Acme Corporation and for the opportunity to work for Chris, her first question was about vacation. She had over ten years with her prior employer and had worked her way up to four weeks of vacation. She had reviewed our policy, which required one full year of work before getting two weeks of vacation, and three weeks didn't come until after five years. She very carefully but deliberately explained that we were about to reap the tangible benefits of all of her years of experience, and she was bringing all those years to apply immediately to our engineering problems. Integrative bargainers have this notion in common; they engage actively in the exchange of information in the belief that information on wants and needs, once exchanged, will facilitate the wants and needs of the other party. Chris (who was still in my office) was doing double backflips and scribbling something about give her whatever she wants.

Without committing an answer, I asked her, what might her second question be? To which she inquired if we had any room to negotiate on her base salary. I thought Chris was going to have a heart attack when I asked Clarice what she had in mind. She responded not with an amount but with a request for something within a range of compensation converting to 5 percent to 7 percent over her initial offer.

This, of course, left us with the opportunity to inquire of her, if we were able to make some adjustment in both of these requests, would we have a deal? I was certain Chris was about to hurt herself.

Equally noncommittal, Clarice answered that it depended on what our adjustments were. (Wow! What presence.) I suggested that I needed to speak to Chris Newboss and get right back to her. She agreed. Chris was exhausted.

We agreed to give her a sidebar agreement that started her with four weeks of annual vacation grandfathering her until she achieved the company service requirement to qualify for that level. Chris, for no specific reason, agreed to split the difference and elevate her base cash compensation by 6 percent. A gesture, I maintain to this day, Clarice totally expected.

Some years later when Clarice and I were working on recruiting engineers for her group, she shared with me in a casual manner that candidates always have alternatives, one of which is to say no thanks to the offer. She admitted she had no other offer in the wings and no intention of staying with her old employer (who did counter, by the way). She had learned this trick from her father, also an engineer, who taught her that injecting ambiguity into the employment process was very beneficial for most candidates. Very wise words.

Clarice Pluperfect was the perfect model for requestive channel negotiation. She was not about to leave the honey pot on the table.

Why is all this important to you? Well, we now have four new concepts firmly in our minds: ultimatum channel, demand channel, requestive channel, and probative inquiry. The first three, as mentioned earlier, are legitimate channels of negotiation that either demand or request more from the employment offer. Probative inquiry is all about clarity. Don't move into negotiations without complete clarity about the offer. Most candidates do well with asking clarity questions but still have difficulty transitioning to a negotiation strategy. My point exactly ... it never hurts to ask.

CHAPTER

5

Anatomy of an Offer

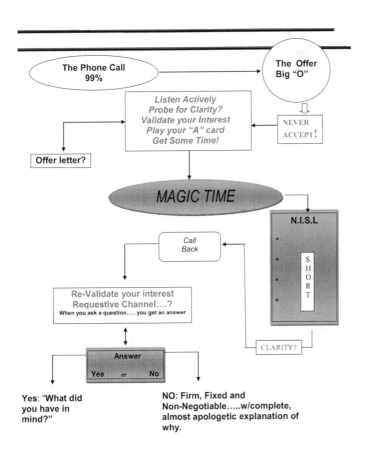

This is the most important chapter in the book; it is where you begin to put RCN to use. First, take some time to look carefully at the anatomy of an offer diagram. While it will be a bit more complex when the opportunity involves relocation (see chapter 9), I have made the diagram intentionally simplistic to make the flow of how it works more user friendly. Simple as it is, please note that at the top it starts with rule number one, which is *never accept the offer when it is presented.* By observing this one simple rule, you automatically put yourself in the world of the 10 percenters. Ninety percent of the population either accepts the offer immediately or they start negotiating immediately, and in my opinion, you should do neither of these. What you do is listen actively by asking questions where you are uncertain or unsure, validate your interest with sincerity, and then indicate that you now have some alternatives to consider, it is an important decision, and you would like some time to consider the offer. You don't need much time; the impact of your response and request will set the stage for negotiations at the very least and possibly set other reactions in motion that will serve you well.

For simplicity sake, the diagram and this narrative ignore the possibility of relocation, which complicates the whole process only modestly but does take more time. The relocation narrative is taken up in detail in chapter 9.

Your offer of employment is delivered by phone most of the time. Sure, there are times when the offer is made on the spot at the conclusion of the interview, is sent in an e-mail message, or occasionally even via overnight express, but in the vast majority of cases, it occurs after the final round of interviews and after the decision makers have had a chance to put their heads together to structure an offer custom designed for you. If you would like a peek under the tent of how that offer is created, see chapter 8.

For the company, this is the really exciting time. By the time the company has decided who they want to hire, they have considered a large number of candidates and conducted a lot of interviewing to get down to a short list. In most cases, the company will have completed the due diligence (reference checking and verification) on their desired candidate before an offer is presented. It is always exciting to get an offer of employment; it is one of life's special moments. You have excelled in the interview and the vetting process, and you have bested the competition. There is just something special about being validated as the chosen one. Both sides are ready to wrap it up and close the deal.

Pause here for a moment.

This is important. It is the only time in the whole book I will suggest that you need to observe only one rule. Here it is again: *never* accept *any* offer of employment when it is presented. *Never.* When you get the offer, validate your interest and show some enthusiasm. Make certain that you ask any immediate questions you have about the terms and conditions of employment. This is not negotiating; this is just probing for clarity. Make certain you completely understand the terms and conditions of the employment offer. By the way, it is okay to request that the offer be put in writing and sent to you. Whether by e-mail or by overnight delivery makes little difference, but it is very important to have a written record of your employment offer.

Occasionally, you may run across a company that is reluctant to send employment offers in writing. Red flag! This is a dying breed of company. Perhaps their reluctance is an indication that they have been stung by putting offers in writing before, and that's another red flag. You still need/want a written record. If this is ever the case, it is perfectly legitimate for you to draft your own offer letter by sending your new supervisor a letter summarizing your version of what you heard in the verbal offer. It is best to copy at least one other person in the company with whom you have interviewed; the HR manager is a good one. Close the letter by saying if there is any material difference in what you have written and what they intended, they should let you know right away. Otherwise, what you put in the letter is what you will use to make your acceptance decision.

Most employers put employment offers in writing because they are after the same thing you are—that is, a documented record of the terms and conditions of employment. But most every employer also wants to reinforce that the offer does *not* create an employment contract and that the resulting employment relationship is at will. Only in America.

So then you say, "Well, I'm excited. This is a wonderful opportunity ... but now I have some alternatives to consider, and I need some time to think it over. Would you mind giving me a few days to consider your offer?" *I suggest no deviation from this course.* It is now time to play the A (alternatives) card *and* get some time. These two techniques together initiate employer uncertainty, putting them in the best possible mind-set for negotiations.

To do this properly, you must do both: mention that you now have alternatives to consider (you *always* have alternatives) and request some time to think it over. Remember any company worth going to work for will give you some time.

You and a few hundred thousand fellow Americans who will receive offers this week hardly ever consider injecting some doubt and ambiguity back into the company. However, that is exactly what you need to do to enhance your negotiation leverage. "I now have some alternatives to consider" is just not a very common response. Inside you are bursting with anxiety, and you are probably highly motivated to get on with the new job, and you can't wait to get this abominable process over with. Remember this: you are always better off starting at a higher salary than a lower one. Everything you receive down the road pyramids off your the starting salary. My friends in the compensation field, those who toil in the total rewards game, actually calculate the sizeable differences in total earnings over a few years just from a modest increase in the base salary when you start. The honey pot is usually left behind because most people don't ask for it.

Actually, you don't need to get much time. The desired effect of playing the A card and getting some time is accomplished in the first few hours, frequently in the first few minutes. How you ask for that time is important. What you say matters. It is a subtle but tactically important step in the process. When a company extends an employment offer, *they want you and they want closure.* The truth is they expect you to accept right there on the phone. Most of the time they get their wish. Based upon my personal experience, fully three-quarters of the time, people accept the offer when it is presented.

I am suggesting that you *do not* give them an answer. Most company representatives are not prepared for you to ask for some time. It is a relatively rare request; it is done only one time in ten. They are much more prepared for you either to negotiate with them right then or accept their offer, right then, right there. Only occasionally do they hear someone ask for some time, and even rarer is that request paired with "I have some alternatives to consider."

Some astute recruiters and/or hiring managers might push back a little, inquiring if there is anything you don't understand about the offer. Some may come right out and ask what other alternatives you are considering and/or why you need more time? After all, the screening process has been long and protracted. Haven't you done all the thinking about it that you need to do? (Note: Headhunters generally work to thwart this negotiations tactic. If you are working through a headhunter, see the final paragraphs of chapter 12 for suggestions.)

Don't cave. Stick to your game plan. You always have alternatives, and you need some time to think it through. Simply say to them: "I can't talk about it specifically, there is an incumbent involved so it is sensitive and confidential." If a company ever says to you, "Sorry, you must accept our offer immediately; we have others waiting in line to choose from" or anything resembling this statement, my advice is to take a pass. Any employer worth working for will give you some time. This is how you might do it:

> "I really appreciate your offer (express thanks), and I am excited about the future. I am sure that I can make a difference at Acme Corporation (validate your interest). This is a big decision for us (it's okay to indicate it is a family decision even if it isn't). I have some alternatives to consider, and I need to think this through (this phrase is mission critical). Would you mind giving me a few days to consider your offer?"

You always have alternatives. Even if you have no other job prospects on the planet and you haven't had another interview in six months, you always have alternatives; one alternative you always have is to say no thanks. Staged this way, you let them think what they will. To them, it most likely means that you have other job alternatives. You did not say that, and you are not lying. You're setting the stage. You're negotiating. This simple phrase plants the seeds of doubt, and it is all you have to say. You don't need much time. Two business days or over a weekend is plenty.

The reason for getting some time is subtle but significant. Like I said earlier, your desired impact on the employer happens right away. This plants the seeds of doubt, and the company will do the rest. The small number of people who ask for some time send the company scrambling for what to do next. Since most people either accept right away or start some form of negotiations right away, most company representatives are a bit unnerved by the uncertainty when a candidate simply indicates he/she has some alternatives to consider and asks for some time to think about it. No immediate demands, certainly no acceptance, just the implication that you have some alternatives to consider. To the company, this just doesn't happen very often.

Take the Sally Acree [#9] example. In my role as recruiter, I went back to the hiring manager and reported that I made the offer to Sally. She seemed to receive it well and seemed enthusiastic, but she said that she had some alternatives to consider and she wanted some time to think it through (planting the seeds of doubt).

Then the hiring manager would start thinking (that's not always a good sign). Before long, the hiring manager would call me and ask, "Why would Sally need time to think it over? After all, she was here for two rounds of interviews, and we talked on the phone several times before and after that. We've checked her references. Presumably she has checked us out ... What could she possibly want to think about?" Then human nature and the seeds of doubt would take over with the hiring manager. Human nature can be a scary thing sometimes. In most cases, human nature weaves a complex web of uncertainty and doubt. The hiring manager starts imagining all the reasons Sally might want to think it over, especially in light of the alternatives she expressed.

The supervisor calls me back again, and now he is certain that she was using our offer as a counter for some other offer she had in her pocket. Or he convinced himself that she was using our offer to get a better package with her current employer. Occasionally, the hiring manager would be so uncomfortable with the ambiguity, he/she would want me to call the candidate back and increase our offer. This before Sally had uttered a single word. Human nature has a dark and suspicious side. By the way, this is precisely the impact you are seeking. Most candidates for employment have no idea that this stuff goes through the mind(s) of the people extending the offer. Most never even consider the strategic importance of patience in the negotiating game.

Playing the A card (alternatives) and getting some time does it all for you. It is like a catalyst you throw into the company caldron; frequently it bubbles up into action without doing anything else. By the way, if this ever happens to you and the company adjusts its offer upwards without you questioning or saying anything, you can credit this technique for that increase. You then have the option of accepting or *asking* for even more from the new offer amount.

Another reason for getting some time has to do with control. The company has been in control of everything up to the moment they extend the employment offer. At that moment, they expect closure, and most of the time they get it. The phone call ends with an acceptance and a start date 80 to 85 percent of the time. The recruiter and the hiring manager enjoy a moment of quick celebration, they note the start date on their calendar, and they are off to their next challenge. Remember—of the 25 percent of people who actually engage in some form of negotiation, many of them start right away, and most of them do it in demand or ultimatum channel. Only 10 percent of people (based upon my observation and analysis) naturally gravitate to requestive channel negotiations.

I am suggesting that you can easily plant the seeds of doubt and inject some ambiguity into this model and get some control of your own. The only time the company is not in control is after they make the offer and before you accept. For a very short time, you are in control. In accepting the offer or demanding more immediately, which happens 90 percent of the time, most people blast right past the opportunity to maximize their employment offer.

To review, when you get the offer, validate your interest, show some enthusiasm, tell them you now have some alternatives to consider, and request some (magic) time. This technique is very subtle and very important.

For the last twenty-plus years, I have coached candidates through the outplacement experience. I have now seen the search for employment through the eyes of the candidate, exactly the opposite vantage point of my previous twenty-plus years as an HR guy. Most applicants never even think about the impact they have on the organization when they tell them they have alternatives to consider and need some time to think about it. This simple but important technique frequently puts the company in a genuinely negotiable frame of mind. It might even create a dialogue they wouldn't have had were it not for these well-chosen words. Minimally, it gives the company pause to think.

You simply let doubt do its thing; human nature's dark, suspicious side starts to alter the company's assessment of its position. The recruiter, the hiring manager, or both start to think that you could say "thanks but no thanks" and turn them down. The company starts to second-guess their offer even before you have asked for anything.

Most organizations are loath to start over. Frequently companies don't have a viable second candidate, having lost all interest in candidates other than their first choice. The natural selection process that companies go through frequently puts considerable distance between the top candidate and other candidates. In any event, most hiring managers are pretty much counting on their top candidate accepting the offer. Alternatively, some organizations go through considerable effort to protect themselves from this vulnerability, and they develop a rich and deep talent pool of candidates for their primary hiring needs. Nevertheless, going through a selection process and identifying a top candidate is a form of commitment, and the employer always wants closure from their top candidate.

Time alone gives the candidate an opportunity to experience a rare and fleeting situational advantage. The candidate is now in control. For the very first time in the entire employment process, the candidate is holding the cards, not the company. The tables will turn soon enough, but during this time, the candidate should create his or her Negotiating Items Short List (NISL); please refer once again to the anatomy of the offer diagram. The NISL is just that, a short list of things that you want to ask for. A higher salary is always on the list; usually it is *last* on the list. There is a reason for that ... your cash compensation is the *most* flexible item in your employment offer. You fill in the NISL items. They can be economic or noneconomic. If you want a different title, now is the time to put it on the list. If you want more vacation or if you want a front-end (signing) bonus or a severance agreement, it goes on the list. If you want more options, more whatever, it goes on the list.

The NISL ultimately has to be a *short* list. That means you can have a few items on it, but it cannot read like a laundry list; it must be short. So after you have created your ultimate wish list, you may have to assign priorities. Which three or four things matter the most to you? If the job is local and does not require relocation, the list might be even shorter. If a move is required, the number of negotiable items goes up a bit.

I counsel my executive outplacement candidates that one of the items on the NISL might be a termination allowance or severance agreement. Very few employment contracts are offered in the States. In fact, the United States is among the least likely countries in the world to offer employment agreements as part of the employment process (see chapter 18). The doctrine of employment at will is alive and well, and almost every domestic employment offer clearly states that it is specifically not a contract for employment. Usually employment agreements are reserved for only top executive talent where the terms and conditions (T&Cs) of employment and termination need to be articulated. Remember—all jobs are temp jobs (see chapter 17). Frequently, severance agreements along with the terms and conditions of employment can be quite adequately spelled out in the offer letter; you do not need an employment agreement for that. While employment agreements may be rare, American firms are still fond of noncompete agreements, arbitration agreements, best and total effort agreements, nonproselytize agreements, secrecy and invention agreements but not many employment agreements. More on this in chapter 18.

During the time you are contemplating, considering, and refining your NISL, it is also a good time to rehearse asking for these things. After all, this is the essence of RCN ... the ask. But before you get to the "ask," you must have all the clarity issues resolved. Getting clarity is a matter of obtaining, reading, and understanding all of the company literature about benefits, policy, and culture. These documents come mostly from the company and should be provided at some point during the recruiting process. However, don't overlook your own research ability. With the convenience of the Internet and social media, you can discover a great deal about the employer's environment before you ever set foot inside the organization. You need all the clarity you can get about what it is like working for this firm.

Asking for clarity is *not* the same as asking for more compensation. Asking for clarity is probative inquiry; it is a communications channel but not a negotiations channel. It is getting basic information. Asking for more money is negotiating, and that comes after your seeds of doubt and your magic time. I have a whole chapter on fit and culture, and you must gather intelligence on your employer from sources other than what they give you. Your own due diligence on the company is important. Understanding the culture of this new organization is instrumental to the values alignment between you and your new employer and ultimately to your success (see chapter 13).

It really should not take you long to come up with your NISL. Hopefully, by the time you arrive at the offer stage, you have had multiple interviews and time also to review the benefits booklets and other assorted policy material that the company has provided you. Don't be timid. Since ERISA was passed, organizations have worked with their benefits providers and attorneys to create summary plan descriptions (SPDs) on every one of their qualified benefits plans. Beware, most of the plans that are ERISA approved are impossible to negotiate because by definition they must be the same in terms of benefit and eligibility for all employees who qualify, and they specifically cannot be designed for the benefit of highly compensated employees. However, as you move up the organizational ladder, you will at some point be able to negotiate a number of nonqualified benefits that are exclusive to executive territory. Consult the appendix for a list of potentially negotiable items. I promise you, at some level of employment within the organization, many if not all the items on this list are negotiable. See what you have in store as you move on up the line?

While you are enjoying the magic time you have so artfully requested, your mention of alternatives is weighing heavily upon the decision makers back at employment central. Organizational reactions vary. Sometimes companies react spontaneously to this information, and sometimes the moguls of talent acquisition patiently bide their time and do nothing. But some things start happening right away.

Case in point, after investing weeks in screening and interviewing a panel of design engineering candidates, narrowing down the field to a short list, carefully checking multiple references, and then selecting her favorite candidate, Richard Woofter (#10), not his real name, the hiring manager, Ingrid, and I created and then extended the employment offer, followed it up in writing, and sent it via FedEx to his home. Ingrid's reaction was very interesting and a great learning experience for me. Her discomfort with what happened next was one that would be played out again and again throughout my recruiting career. Ingrid was one of our top engineering directors, and the news that her prize BSEE candidate with five well-spent and directly transferrable years at a respected competitor had requested a few days' time to think about our offer was almost bizarre. When I reported that he had enthusiastically received the verbal offer but mentioned that he had some alternatives to consider and needed some time to think over the offer, she moved immediately into high gear. "What alternatives?" she demanded to know. Did he mean other employment offers? Did he mean a possible counter from his current employer? She was inconsolable. Ingrid almost went into meltdown right before my eyes. I understood that she did not want to lose this candidate, but her intolerance for the ambiguity of the situation was a side of Ingrid I had never seen before. My attempts to assuage her discomfort were fruitless. Before the day was out, she was back in my office reexamining every aspect of our offer. "Should we suggest a more appropriate title and position on the technical ladder?" she demanded to know. "Did we offer enough money? We have some room to move within the salary range. Should we call him back and make a higher offer?" She was absolutely frenetic.

I don't know if Richard was a sophisticated enough negotiator to intentionally set these wheels in motion within our company; probably not, he had only five years of total heads-down engineering design experience at only one employer. Right or wrong, I finally convinced Ingrid that he asked for the time in good faith, and we needed to honor his request. In reality, it was my job to understand what barriers stood in the way of his acceptance of our offer. If I had been doing my job correctly, I should have known the answers before we made our offer. Lesson well learned, and I never made that kind of mistake again. It was all I could do to dissuade Ingrid from calling the candidate and sweetening the offer before he had asked for a single concession.

As it turned out, he accepted the offer as presented after five days to think about it, including a weekend. Also, as it turned out, the alternatives that he needed to consider involved a family pet who was suffering a terminal illness, and his children were very emotionally attached, creating a very difficult time for the family. He wasn't sure that accepting a new job with all of its additional stress and responsibility was a wise family decision. After discussions with his wife and the children and taking a few days to think about it, he called back and accepted the offer gratefully and graciously without any negotiations. Little did Richard know that he could have negotiated for significantly more had he only asked. Richard had no appreciation or awareness of the angst that his actions would create within the hiring management of our company. However, it made an indelible impression upon me. The ambiguity that Richard had introduced had indeed put the hiring manager and the recruiter (me) in an uncomfortable position.

This dynamic reappeared time after time in my personal experience, and it goes on within all companies at some level, but the opportunity to introduce the same ambiguity escapes most candidates who simply accept the job when offered. Don't *ever* do that. Validate your interest and show some enthusiasm but never accept the offer when it is first delivered. Instead say, "I have some alternatives that I need to consider, and I wonder if you would mind giving us a few days to consider your offer?" Then stop. Any company worth working for will give you some time, and this time is magic because of what it does internally within the company.

Had Richard seized the moment and simply asked if there was any room for negotiation, he would have started from a higher base and pyramided it upward over time. The higher you can negotiate your starting salary, the better off you are down the road when increases (usually in percentages) come along.

While the company goes through these internal stress issues, you should be thinking about the things that are negotiable and what should go on your NISL. If you are being offered a ranged job, then there is almost always some room for the company to sweeten the base cash compensation. If you are being offered a rated job, then it is unlikely that there will be any room to negotiate the starting rate, but it still doesn't hurt to ask. Whether ranged or rated, it will be difficult to change the benefits side of the offer. Participation eligibility on the 401(k) is not going to change, nor will the parameters of the major medical plan where ERISA is involved, or the bonus participation where the company is highly structured and has a lot of precedent about bonus entitlement. Sometimes the title is negotiable, and if a change in title is important to you, now is the time to ask if it can be changed. Sometimes you can negotiate a sidebar agreement on vacation eligibility or even a sign-on bonus. Remember when you call back to make no demands and certainly no ultimatums, just requests. When you make a request in a proper and respectful manner, you get an answer. It may be no, but then again it might be yes. Importantly, offers aren't pulled back or rescinded when you are in requestive channel, and most of the time, something on your short list will resonate with the powers that be, and something will be granted.

When you ask, you will receive an answer. Asking is vastly different from making a demand and worlds apart from issuing an ultimatum, both of which are legitimate channels of negotiation that frequently fail. Ultimatum channel fails more than demand channel, but both fail enough for you to be very careful when using either one of these channels. Requestive channel negotiation (RCN), when done right, has never failed to produce an answer— yes or no, but your offer never disappears even when it is a no answer. Sometimes a yes is disguised as a "Well, what did you have in mind?" and when presented with that question, which happens frequently, you need to remind yourself to stay in requestive channel. You should not answer that inquiry with a specific amount. Why? Because that would move you into demand channel. Always answer this question with a range. Leave the final decision up to the company; they love being in charge.

Example: Suppose the offering manager has presented you with a base cash compensation offer of $75,000 per year. Let's say you were hoping for at least $72,000 to $74,000. "Wow," you say. "That is more than I expected." Even though the initial offer exceeds what you hoped for, you still observe rule number one: Do not accept the offer when presented ... ever. You also don't start negotiating during that call. You validate your interest and play the A card and get a couple of days to think about the opportunity. This will be hard. There is already more money on the table than you expected, but you exercise some patience. You consider your NISL. Then, at the appointed time, you call back and revalidate your interest in the position and ask if there is any flexibility in the base cash offer of $75,000?

Remember—when there is a question mark (?) at the end of the sentence, you are in requestive channel ... clear sailing. If there is a period (.) at the end of the sentence, you are in demand channel ... danger. If there is an exclamation point (!) at the end of the sentence, then you are most likely in ultimatum channel ... downright scary.

So if you ask if there is any flexibility to negotiate the base cash compensation, be prepared for an answer. It might be, "Well not much actually, but what did you have in mind?" This is not quite a yes, but it is much better than "Well, actually we don't have any flexibility. It's the most we can do under the current business circumstances." That is probably a no. In any event, do not answer this question with a specific number. If you put a specific number on the table, ask yourself, "How far away am I from putting a period on the end of the sentence instead of a question mark?" If you answer, "I was actually hoping for $78,000," you have just slipped into demand channel ... danger.

Better to put another range on the table and reformat it into the form of a question: "Would it be possible to get the offer somewhere in the high seventies or low eighties?" This keeps you in RCN, but please remember whenever you put a range out there, you have also said that the lower end of your range would be acceptable to you. So if they come back with a $78,000 offer, you need to be ready to accept. Since almost every department manager is responsible for effectively managing the departmental expense line, it is unlikely that manager will come back to you with anything over your range minimum, but stranger things have happened, and obviously it doesn't hurt to ask.

Whatever else may be on your NISL should be requested of the hiring authority in similar "requestive" fashion. I suggest that you save base cash compensation for last because it represents the most flexible part of your offer, presuming that we are dealing with a ranged job and not a rated job.

Almost all formal compensation structures are designed so that midpoint is the actual paid rate of fully qualified personnel from competitive companies as established by detailed analysis of survey data. A more detailed discussion of how these numbers are arrived at would bore you to death and add little to your negotiation expertise. The important part to remember is midpoint is hard to exceed for a new employee and generally requires the HR professional *and* the hiring manager to crawl on their hands and knees across a carpet filled with tacks and broken glass in the president's office to seek permission to go over midpoint. It can be done in certain circumstances, but it just isn't in the cards usually.

If you are being hired by a smaller company without any formal compensation structure, the exact same rules apply: affordability and prior compensation and internal compatibility are the big three. However, in the absence of formal structure like job evaluation and salary ranges and compensation surveys, affordability is determined by what the company paid your predecessor. If you are replacing Jennifer, affordability is determined by what the organization paid Jennifer before she left the company. If they paid Jennifer $55,000 to do the production expeditor job, then chances are her replacement will be paid about the same amount … somewhere around $55,000, probably less to start.

Fine-tuning of your offer is always made by your compensation history, and employers put blanks on application forms because they want to know precisely what you have been earning. If you are replacing Jennifer and you have a salary history recently topping out at $47,000, your offer will be biased (downward) by this number. If you have recently made $57,000, the same variable is at work; your offer will be biased (upward) by that number. In the former case, the bias will be to lower the offer but still give you a slight raise. In the latter case, the bias will be higher with a further fine-tuning depending upon how you were recruited, your current employment situation, and the company need for your talents in the future. The third criteria will probably never be revealed to you, but know this, there are people in the HR department whose job is to make sure internal compatibility is not upset by any new employee coming in and creating a pay inequity.

Ultimately, ranged positions have some built-in flexibility by their very structure, and you can usually negotiate a little bit more by asking the right questions and staying in requestive channel. But you won't know unless you ask.

CHAPTER 6

The Repetitive Chapter—
It's Worth Repeating

To reiterate, there is only one rule of salary negotiations according to Jack. That rule is *never* accept the offer when it is given to you. It is okay—in fact it is recommended—that you show some enthusiasm, because you want the company to know that you are genuinely excited about the opportunity. It is okay to ask for clarity on any aspects of the offer that are not clear to you. It is okay to request that the offer be put in writing and sent to you by e-mail or snail mail.

Then it is okay to play your A card—A for alternatives—and guess what? You always have alternatives, and you want to find a way to tell the person extending your offer that you have alternatives because alternatives plant the seeds of doubt into the company. You don't have to do a single thing to make that seed grow and work for you; the recruiter/hiring manager will do it all for you. So mention that you have some alternatives to consider and you need some time to think it over ... perfect!

Now, these two things (A card and time) working in tandem are the magic potion that most candidates never even think about. Most breeze right by this in the heated rush to extinguish that burning desire to get this over with. So most candidates accept the offer presented. My advice to you is *don't do that.* Remember rule number one: never accept an offer when it is given.

Now, at this point you have not negotiated a thing. Your offer call is never a negotiating call. It might serve to clarify some things and answer some specific questions, but it is not a negotiating conversation. The sole purpose of mentioning alternatives and getting some time is to plant the seed of doubt by injecting some ambiguity back into the employer.

What happens when you mention that you have some alternatives to think about and request some time? Well, it varies a bit, but the seeds of doubt start to spread almost right away. The first thing the offering representative does, be they the HR recruiter or hiring manager, is have a conversation with the other decision makers and spread the word: "Well, the offer went fine, and she sounded sincere and enthusiastic, and she asked a couple of questions about the benefit plans ... but then she said she had some alternatives to consider and requested some time to think it through." And then: "I wonder if she has another offer," or "I wonder if her company has given her a counter offer," or "I wonder what alternatives she means."

The seeds of doubt start to work right away; it doesn't take long. I have story after story about the various reactions of hiring managers after the seeds of doubt take hold and ambiguity displaces certainty that their prime candidate is a shoe-in for acceptance. That ambiguity ranges from "Do you suppose we made a good enough offer?" and, "We still have some room to move on the offer, don't we?" to even, "Let's call her back and make her a higher offer." Some hiring managers are less concerned and willing to sit it out; after all, "It is an important decision, and she deserves some time to think about it." But most start to worry, and that worry, that uncertainty at the very least, puts the company in a mood to reconsider the offer. And *that*, ladies and gentlemen, is why we have rule number one and its supporting cast of the A card and magic time.

This is *so* important I wanted to say it again. There! I've said it again. All you have to do is ask.

CHAPTER 7

Three Promises and Roger Graham Too

Utilizing requestive channel negotiations is a matter of choice. It is up to you. However, if your situation warrants utilizing ultimatum channel, it may just be the way to go. If your personality dictates that you need to be a demand channel negotiator, then so be it. But my personal favorite and the one I think makes the most sense for most people in transition is requestive channel. If I can reach just a few of the 75 percenters, I know it will make a difference in their lives.

It took me years to isolate and analyze the various channels. There are three main reasons for that. First, I am a slow learner. Someone else probably could have done it in half the time. Second, I wasn't looking for patterns, so I didn't see any. Third, I didn't know then that I would be writing a book about this stuff. It wasn't until I began the second half of my career working with people in career transition that I started to focus on assisting individuals move through career change in the most efficient and effective way and to their greatest advantage.

Lots of people change jobs every year. Think about it. If we have 140 million working people in the labor market, and if we had average turnover of only 18 percent to 20 percent (it is actually much higher according to the DOL), that is twenty-five to twenty-eight million people changing jobs and an equal number of opportunities to become a 10 percenter.

All together, I figure I have hired or had a hand in hiring nearly twenty thousand people in my career. That's a lot of people. In order to hire that many people, I assure you that I have interviewed a lot more. I have also made more offers than that as well. Believe it or not, not everyone accepted my gracious and thoughtful offers of employment; some, for totally inexplicable reasons, actually turned me down. Some didn't work out. Some were countered by their company (that usually told me I had a good one). Some I rescinded. So to get over twenty thousand hits, I talked with a lot more. But when it comes to you, your circumstances are unique. No other human being is quite like you, and you will go about this in your own way. If you are currently employed, the circumstances are different from if you were just laid off. Your actual leverage varies with your circumstances.

I know negotiating your personal compensation is not easy. When I started with Firestone in the employment department, I had an initial hiring quota of fifty people a week. Back then it was not a particularly sophisticated employment process. But this coupled with my other hiring experiences were and still are the behavioral laboratory in which I cultivated the notion that there is no downside to asking for more. So I want to move some of that great silent, nonnegotiating 75 percent majority of candidates toward an awareness that it is okay to ask.

If you apply yourself to learning requestive channel negotiations and then actually apply the techniques, like I said in the overview at the beginning, I will make you three promises. Promise number one is that if there is more to be gotten, you will get all or some of it through RCN. In other words, you will *maximize* your offer. Remember—I started this book in the opening chapter with the notion that for negotiations to work, there must be room for flexibility in the compensation system, and there must be a willingness to engage in the negotiation process. Both aspects must work together. It matters not that there is a lot of room to negotiate if the candidate fails to ask for it.

Promise number two is that RCN is a *no-risk* technique if you engage it correctly. I know of no examples where a candidate had his or her offer rescinded as a result of engaging in this technique. More importantly, many companies recognized both the employee and the technique as a living example of a great personal style. As an employer, I also held great expectations that the employee would represent the company in similar fashion.

Keep in mind that there are three legitimate channels of negotiations with which to engage a prospective employer: RCN, DCN, and UCN. Of these three, requestive channel is the only one with zero risk. Demand channel has markedly more risk and results in both lost offers and failed negotiations about 15 to 20 percent of the time. Ultimatum channel results in the most frequent occasion of both lost offers and failed negotiations 50 to 60 percent of the time. Risk is always inherent in the negotiation process, and in the case of counter demands and ultimatums, employers are free to seek other alternatives to fill their available jobs. We know this.

Asking a question, however, has no known risk because questions get answers, and questions are not prejudicial if tendered appropriately. You know you are in requestive channel when you structure the sentence to end with a question mark. Stay in questioning mode when you ask for more.

Promise number three is peace of mind. Even if you get nothing tangible for engaging in RCN, you still have your original offer. That is why it is no risk. Your original offer is still there even if the employer says no to your request for more. You will then have the peace of mind of knowing that no one could have negotiated a better offer from the company for this position at this point in time.

Interestingly, over 90 percent of the time, those who engage in these techniques actually receive something tangible. That means they increase their offer of compensation, front-end bonus, variable compensation, title, vacation accrual, perquisite structure, or some improvement from the company in the terms and conditions originally offered. Only about 9 percent of candidates experience no tangible adjustment in the terms and conditions (T&C) of their original offer. Even they enjoy the peace of mind knowing that their offer is the best it is going to be at this time, which, as you will soon learn, opens up the possibility of negotiating for the future.

So when you use RCN in response to your next employment offer, my three promises are: You will maximize your offer. You will not put your offer in jeopardy. You will enjoy the peace of mind of knowing you just negotiated the best possible package available for you from this company at this point in time.

Perhaps more important is the lasting impression you make on your new employer. I remember from engaging in the hiring process with people who exhibited these behaviors that I actually enjoyed dealing with them. They represented their interests well and did so in a friendly, engaging, and yet highly professional manner. They did so with a style and demeanor that was easy to like.

It took me a number of years working with people to put the correct labels on these behaviors and then to associate the technique of having alternatives and then requesting some time to think over the offer—and even longer to figure out ways to suggest that you too can do this and to write this book.

Let me spend some time explaining why I can make such confident promises. I know for certain that these techniques work, and I know the positive impression that they leave on the people you will work with inside the company. In addition to my own personal experience with hiring lots of folks into some of America's finest organizations, I have had the added experience of working with thousands of people in career transition (outplacement). After leaving corporate America with over two decades in the human resources trade, I have spent another two decades plus in career transition work. First I was with a small boutique outplacement firm in Phoenix that specialized in middle- and upper-management employees. Then I opted to take a risk and became a founding partner in a similar organization and put my name on the door. Any way you look at it, my entire work life has been with individuals in some phase of the employment process. I don't take these three promises lightly. They work, and they have a measurable ROI, but you have to do your part—you have to ask.

Take the case of Roger Graham [#11], a college-educated electrical engineer from a solid Midwestern school with over five years of experience as an engineering manager supervising a team of double Es working on micro-circuitry in the semiconductor business. His company first moved all stateside manufacturing and production to the Pacific Rim, and then his company was merged with another high-tech firm in order to achieve even more economies of scale. Roger was not selected to manage any of the post-merger engineering departments and then was laid off. He received two of life's major hardship lessons back to back. This was the first time this had ever happened to him, and he was overwhelmed with possibilities for disaster. He was in his late thirties with three young children, and his wife was a part-time teacher with a small income that went more for mad money than the necessities of family support.

There was a lot of pressure on Roger, most of it self-imposed, to find something quickly. Fortunately, he was given a modest severance program and outplacement assistance; that is how I met him. Roger had a lot of good things going for him, and he liked the management track he had been on and envisioned himself as a capable leader of technical people. He wanted upward mobility and had aspirations of becoming a top-level engineering leader someday. Fortunately for Roger, he was also resilient, confident, and well grounded.

Roger had a strong technical background and presented well; he secured interviews with three different firms rather quickly. The first two did not get to the offer stage, but he reached the short list with the third company and was asked to provide references, always a good sign. Companies don't invest the time to check references unless they are seriously interested in the candidate. We had worked out his references in advance—two bosses, two peers, and two subordinates (see chapter 11). After the HR department vetted these, he was advised that they were making him an offer. This offer turned out to be $5,000 more than he was expecting and considerably more than he was making before he was laid off. He was understandably euphoric and couldn't wait to share the news with his family. Since he was a graduate of the Leathers

Milligan Industrial-Strength School of Career Transition, he had observed rule number one and played his A card. He had validated his interest in the job, mentioned that he had some alternatives to consider, and requested a few days to think over the offer. He had followed his negotiation training technique to the letter, but it was awkward for him, and every instinct was telling him to accept the offer and get back to work.

Now this is a decision point, perhaps just like one that you will experience at some point in the future. Great company, great job, great boss, great offer exceeding your expectations. "Why bother with negotiations? All these terms are acceptable. Let's do this." The very next day, he was ready to cut the magic time short, call the new boss, accept the job, and get on board. So we had a talk about maximizing, about no risk, about peace of mind, and nothing dissuaded him from his intentions until we spoke about the notion of what pyramiding his compensation would mean if he started from an even higher salary. I got out some paper and a pencil and drew up the X, Y axis and drew the estimated income line over the next ten years based upon his current offer. Maybe the engineer in him took over. When I used the same diagram and showed him what a difference it would make over that same ten-year period if he started at $3,000 or $5,000 or $7,000 higher, he paused. When he saw the change in the curve of the total income line, realizing that all future increases would be leveraged from a higher base, it was like a lightning rod within his engineering mind.

The next two days were sheer agony for Roger and his wife, but we waited it out, and when the appointed time came, he made the call to the new boss and stuck closely to his practiced script. He validated his continued interest in the job and asked if there was any wiggle room in the salary offer. He had cut his NISL to only one item—base cash compensation. The boss responded with, and Roger remembered these words precisely, "Maybe a little. What's it gonna take to get you?" Roger answered appropriately with a requested range that was $5,000 to $7,000 higher, and the boss immediately opted to split the difference and raised his prior offer by another $6,000 on the spot and in the same conversation. Roger was elated. Had he not asked, he would not have received. They agreed on a starting date, and then Roger and his bride celebrated happily.

Working with Roger was a pleasure. He had a great education and background, he did all his preparation and homework, and he took well to coaching. He presented well and interviewed well. He reluctantly but enthusiastically embraced RCN, and it paid off. If nothing else had changed but receiving regular and ordinary increases over that ten years, it would have made over $70,000 difference in Roger's total wealth accumulation. As things worked out, he had two promotions within the first five years, and he wrote me a note after the second one and said that he never forgot the lesson he learned, and he applied RCN on each of those promotions and was successful in obtaining "a little more" each time … just by asking!

Throughout my experiences in the career transition field, I have been testing and fine-tuning these techniques. In addition to Roger Graham, there are thousands of others who have benefited by this technique.

Utilizing RCN does not make $150,000 offers out of $100,000 offers, but it does yield 5 to 10 percent increases in offers regularly. These techniques also add vacation, increase bonuses, create signing bonuses, add to title and role clarity, accelerate compensation reviews, add to or elevate perquisites, and generally provide significant tangible benefit to the people who have studied, practiced, and applied these simple principles.

If you will do that, apply these simple principles, you too can enjoy the benefits that will accrue to you. As with many of life's major revelations, the answers are actually quite simple and straightforward and frequently right in front of us—a respectful but powerful intervention in the negotiation process where you represent yourself in a manner that makes a lasting and positive impression upon your prospective employer and simultaneously puts money in your pocket. Not a bad combination of events and so simple to do, but you have to ask.

CHAPTER

8

How Employment Offers Are Formulated

Three concepts triangulate your job offer with most employers. Your employment offer is formulated from these three concepts: (1) affordability, (2) compensation history, and (3) internal compatibility. These three provide the framework that most employers use to create your ranged offer. Before I explain each of these in detail, let's review the context of your employment offer.

The default mode established in chapter 2 of this book is that there are only two kinds of jobs, rated and ranged. That model continues to work well to explain how employment offers are put together. But upstream from that, let's start with the whole notion of work and its place in our lives. There are, as of this writing, about 310 million people legally living in the United States. As with most developed nations, there is an observed trend that the mechanisms that move the national economy generally support a working population somewhere just under one half of the population. So it stands to reason that the 140 million people in the American civilian, nonfarm, nonmilitary work force are fairly representative of this developed nation club. If you are in this labor force, or thinking about or wanting to be in this labor force, I am hopeful that this book will be of some lasting benefit to you.

If you are not in that labor force, you are probably not reading this book, and the message here doesn't matter. However, to the lesser half of our population to whom work is a matter of sustaining a certain lifestyle, knowing how your employment offer is created is a worthwhile piece of knowledge because frequently you have influence and some degree of control over what that offer looks like. Employment offers are not created in vacuum.

Most employees haven't a clue how their specific employment offer was created, and they don't lose much sleep over the issue either. But then, here you are, reading this book because you are curious about what goes on that initiates all this fuss about negotiations and compounding wealth and honey pots.

Long before anyone gets that phone call with a very personal, custom designed and scientifically formulated, nutritionally enriched offer of employment, a lot has happened. It begins with a large funnel of possibilities and works through an influential alchemy of industry, geography, technology, politics, whimsy, knowledge, skill, education, geophysics, logistics, culture, finance, intuition, time, religion, affluence, influence, preference, serendipity, and occasionally the phase of the moon. Out the narrow end of the funnel emerges the terms and conditions of employment that then get presented to you as an employment offer. An employment offer is an invitation to a relationship. A relationship that is guaranteed to affect change in every aspect of your life. Jobs do that.

Much has been written about the importance of work in our culture, and the collective weight of that information indicates that work always registers somewhere in the top five most important realms of our lives. This is true even if you are not in the labor force: Personal, professional, family, financial, and spiritual issues are consistently the top five and all are interconnected. Things related to work are mostly in the professional sector, but like the others, it too is interwoven with everything else. Statistically speaking, most of us are not born into wealth of a magnitude that sustains us without work. Even those who are in that rare air of economics, work and the notion of making a contribution is a motivational drive that comes from inside, and in varying degrees we are all born with it. Maximizing the economic and the overall welfare derived from your work, whatever that might be, is what this book is all about.

Hopefully, the employer you are considering joining has job descriptions in place. Requesting a job description is okay. Do it. These job duties have an economic value to the employer, and that value is expressed in the compensation and benefits package you are provided as fair exchange for your work.

Having said all that …

Rated jobs: As you know by now, the essential truth about rated jobs is that they are nonnegotiable. Rated jobs have a predetermined specific pay rate at entry. Most rated jobs are part of an already existing hierarchical relationship and paid rates that are tied together by tradition or agreement or both. Most government jobs fit into this category, and while there is some elasticity at higher levels, for the most part, they are rated jobs.

Ranged jobs: Most of America's working population (fortunately) works in ranged jobs with some flexibility around the concept of base cash compensation (pay). It is these jobs that are target-rich environments inviting your personal negotiations skill to be put to the test. While ultimatum and demand channel have their rightful place when the circumstances warrant, my personal favorite is requestive channel negotiation regardless of your situation and your personality.

Whether you are being promoted, coming in from another division of the same company, or coming in as a brand-new employee, requestive channel works. As I have said many times to satisfied clients, it is better that the honey pot resides in your house.

As it relates to you personally, and presuming you are applying for a ranged position, your offer formulation starts with your employment application. Most employment professionals know that your resume is a marketing document, but your employment application is a promise with serious consequences for misrepresentation. When you sign your application, you make a promise of truthfulness and give the company authorization to check and verify. That is why HR departments everywhere browbeat candidates not to use "see resume" in any part of the application process. At the end of most every employment application, there is such a promissory statement.

On that original application, you likely had a blank to fill out that dealt with your starting and ending salary for every position in recent history. Always be truthful because a misstatement (falsification) here will ruin your credibility as a candidate and wreck your employment chances with that employer.

The first of the three issues that formulate your offer is where you will fit in the pay range. It is what compensation professionals call the affordability issue. Affordability is the employer's ability to pay within a certain pay range for that job. This translates to what the company has to say about the value of the job you are going to be doing.

There are at least three main avenues of thought about affordability. The first and most common among organizations with some structure has to do with the range of pay (minimum to maximum) within the employer's compensation system. If they have job descriptions and a formal evaluation process and grades and ranges (minimum, midpoint, maximum), then the affordability issue is dictated by the grade and pay range of the vacant job. Usually the hiring range is between the minimum and the midpoint, and this defines the flexibility the company has built into the compensation structure. The second (and opposing) avenue of thought has to do with the opposite of all that structure stuff and a reliance upon market data. This presumes the company has access to appropriate market data and can use that information to determine a legitimate pay range for your services based upon what others are paying for similar services. The third avenue of thought is the most common among small and entrepreneurial companies; the affordability issue is determined by what was paid to the prior occupant of the job. If your predecessor Sally made $47,000 in the job, chances are that the target to hire someone replacing Sally will be somewhere around $47,000, probably less to start. All three of these variations are examples of a ranged job.

The second factor that influences the formulation of your offer is your compensation history. What have you done and what were you paid to do it? Never lie about your compensation. I am reminded about an embarrassing experience when I worked for a large government contractor that included a contractual responsibility to the US government to validate all salary histories that candidates provided. In fact, we had a large sign in the employment lobby attesting to the requirement for documentation of previous income. We were well into the recruiting and due diligence phase with a senior-level manager and on the threshold of making him an offer. His experience was mostly commercial nongovernmental employment. At some point just before extending the offer, I requested a copy of his last paystub to verify his compensation. Either he had not read our sign or didn't believe it. In any event, his jaw dropped, and the blood drained from his face, and I thought he was going to faint. He had no idea that he would be challenged on this and that we would actually ask for documented proof of his claimed income. Since much of your offer creation is based upon your previous compensation, this is an important issue. The US government was absolutely inflexible in this requirement and had audit points built in to assure contract compliance. Well, he hummed and hawed and stalled for a few days, but it turned out he had overstated his current salary by over 20 percent. He was surprised we asked but still expected to be hired. This breech in honesty destroyed his chances of employment with us, and he went away ashamed, compromised, and with a bit of a sullied reputation, caught in a lie.

It is legitimate for any company, not just government contractors, to ask for proof of prior income. Be prepared to substantiate your compensation claim and don't lie.

The third and usually the final factor in formulating your offer is how you align (compare) to others already in the company. This factor emerges in organizations of sufficient size and structure where this concept actually matters. The company will analyze the new employee's suggested salary within the range on a percentile comparison with all other employees in the grade and range. This is an equity check, and it is a formal process. No company wants to immediately create an obvious inequity between the new employee and those employees in similar jobs with more service. It is not good employee relations, and it creates employee resentment.

Guess what? Employees actually talk with each other about their compensation and have a legally protected right to do so.

Contrary to popular corporate belief, employees may discuss their salaries with one another, in spite of policies to keep salary information confidential. I am still amazed at the level of corporate ignorance around such issues because federal labor law gave all employees covered by the National Labor Relations Act (most everyone) the absolute legal right to engage in protected, concerted activity for their mutual gain way back in 1935. Discussing your salary with another employee is clearly a protected, concerted activity under the law. Companies that see fit to actually discipline employees for discussing "confidential salary information" are violating federal law. A five-minute call to any employment attorney usually changes the corporate mind-set (and policy) on this issue.

So there you have it, the Full Monty revealed about how employment offers are created. So how does all this fit into your negotiation strategy? The whole notion of RCN is not to double your salary; it is about working within that range of flexibility in ranged jobs and appropriately asking for more. Requesting a modest amount (usually between 3 and 8 percent) is a high percentage play, and having the money in your wallet is better than leaving it in the company wallet. If you ask and you get this "modest," amount and you do the math about starting from a higher place and pyramiding that with every salary increase that follows (the honey pot), you will be amazed at how much more wealth you create for yourself and your family by just asking.

CHAPTER

9

Relocation and the Negotiation Process

When the ideal job is three states away or around the world, it complicates the negotiations process. Of all the things to consider, the most basic is whether or not this job serves your career path in a way that makes all the disruption that accompanies moving make sense. Sometimes moving is the only alternative, and we have to go where the opportunity presents. Certain professions have embraced this notion in ways that make moving a regular and ordinary fact of life. Other career paths and personal choice make moving a rare and scary thing to be avoided if possible.

The military, for instance, is a career choice where moving must be embraced. I grew up as an army brat, and moving was not only part of the regular routine; it was an expected and exciting part of growing up. My mother was a great army wife and couldn't wait to pick up and move across the state or around the world; she embraced the realities of army life and thrived on change. Government positions in the State Department relocate professionals all over the globe on a regular basis. Just as often, more so recently, family life in one place has become more important than ever, and moving is a sacrifice that fewer and fewer professionals are choosing to make.

There is much to be said on the positive side of relocation and an equal amount of negative implications as well. But whether the job is ideal and relocation is appropriate or perhaps it is the only job left on the planet, when relocation is required, it is best approached with a positive spirit of adventure. If there is one thing I learned from moving fifteen times in my first seventeen years, it is this: If the family unit is cohesive and mutually supportive, you can be happy anywhere. If the family unit is fractured and conflict ridden, relocation will only serve to amplify those difficulties.

Not everyone approaching the relocation challenge is married with kids. DINKs (dual income, no kids) are often provided with career opportunities that require moving. Likewise, simpros (single, mobile professionals) face the possibility that relocation across town or to another state or around the world makes perfectly good career sense. I want you to know that negotiating the terms and conditions can make otherwise unacceptable career choices highly lucrative and perfectly appropriate and culturally rewarding.

Whatever your situation, when relocation becomes a career choice, it is best done with the expectation that negotiating the terms of that relocation are a part of expected behavior. Your new employer wants you relocated into the new opportunity with the greatest possibility for success. Most employers openly embrace the notion that removing obstacles to success is good business.

Relocation to a distant place, whether married with kids or single and mobile, requires some time to explore the new community, and most employers over the past two decades have learned that utilization of a professional relocation company enhances success significantly. Relocation assistance is big business; there is even a professional association of relocation people. If it isn't already a built-in part of your offer, go ahead and ask for the assistance of a relocation company at the first indication that the employer is seriously interested in your candidacy. Don't wait until the offer stage, but if you get to the offer and you have not been provided these services, please ask and do so *before* you get into the negotiation stage.

Working with a professional relocation firm is not like being driven around the area looking at homes by a real estate agent. Relocation companies that are doing it right for individuals and families begin well before you visit the area by contacting you and getting as much information from you about your needs as you are comfortable with sharing. "Relo firms," as they are known in the trade, will pick you up at the airport or hotel and provide a complete briefing about the local community, its history, demographics, and commuting patterns, along with very valuable insider information that is not readily available to you without a lot of research. They will provide you with a complete and well-documented package of cultural, historical, and demographic overview of the area that you can take with you for review later.

Companies know that the right relo firm can make or break the employment decision of a candidate, so when it is important to them for you to say yes, most employers will pull out all the stops and frequently will involve themselves in the program, for either a dinner or lunch to get direct feedback and make certain that all is going well. Make no mistake; the relo firm has a vested interest in your decision to accept the opportunity, and they provide a lot of feedback to the employer, so be careful about your dialogue, as your representative is frequently a direct line of information back to the company. Keep in mind who is paying them. They make their money in one of two ways; they are either paid directly by the company, or they are paid by a revenue-sharing agreement through your purchase of real estate.

If you get an offer involving relocation and you haven't really examined the new community where you will be living, by all means get a trip scheduled *before* you begin negotiating your offer. While relocation complicates the process, it does not change the basic steps you see in chapter 5, anatomy of an offer. Nothing changes the number-one rule: never accept an offer when it is given. You always validate your interest, say you have some alternatives to consider, and then you request some time. The magic of introducing ambiguity back into the company cannot be overstated, and any company worth going to work for will give you some time.

If relo is involved, it is perfectly okay to indicate that you will need time to visit the new community (accompanied by your spouse, partner, or significant other) and determine if that location will work for you *and them* as a family and as a professional. Spouses, particularly if they have their own careers, and your children are the ones who will face the brunt of the change to their lives. You have an exciting new job to go off to every day, with a built-in set of contacts and friends and challenges. Your spouse has to create his or her new environment, and together the two of you have to find the stores and churches, doctors and schools, bowling alleys, bagels, and new friends. You should be as sensitive as possible to these new challenges. As excited as you are to get busy in the new job, you must remember much of your new world is artificially created around you by the job. Your spouse and kids have to create most everything on their own, and that is a whole different challenge. This enculturation of your family is mission critical to the success of the relocation, doubly so if your relocation is international. Relocation companies know it, employers know it, and you should know it. This is another reason relo companies can be of such a great service.

The generally accepted wisdom in deciding the economics of a new location is that the two big differences are real estate cost and taxes. Everything else that goes into the daily routine will fit into what is generally called the "market basket" of daily life, but the taxation structure of the various states, counties, municipalities, and even home owners associations varies greatly region to region. Likewise, real estate in Petaluma, California, is vastly different from Poughkeepsie and from Peoria, Pulaski, and Pittsburgh. So in addition to whatever relo support you get, you want to get on your search engine and compare both the tax structure and the real estate cost of your new location. If your tax adviser is affiliated with a national firm, he or she can get you the tax differences very easily. Alternatively, check out www.retirementliving.com and click on taxes by state.

The purpose of the initial house-hunting trip with your spouse is paradoxically not to find a suitable home; that usually comes later. The primary purpose is simply to get a good feel for the area, the geography, the culture, the weather, the socioeconomic aspects, and the whole ambiance of this potential new home. You want to come away from your visit with a feeling that either it will work for you or it won't. If the place is not for you, no amount of negotiating is going to make you see the area in a different light. If it is not to be, it is best to extricate yourself from further consideration in the most professional manner possible. Never burn a bridge, and the way you handle feedback to the employer about why this location does not work for you could very well affect some future opportunity. So be careful and considerate and thoughtful about your dialogue with everyone involved.

Here are some issues about relocating you may want to focus on:

- taxes (all kinds) and possible gross-up of relo expenses
- difference per square foot in the cost of housing
- moving of household goods and costs (insurance too)
- health care coverage and differences
- temporary living and temporary storage
- settling-in costs
- costs related to the sale and purchase or lease of home
- seasonal cost differences (if any)
- commuting patterns and times
- geopolitical and cultural realities
- long-term strategic plans for your new town, city, or community
- walkability of the new neighborhood
- transportation systems and costs (public alternatives, routes, times, expenses)
- schools and any special educational needs
- avocational and recreational alternatives
- clubs and hobbies
- spousal employment opportunities and spousal career transitional support
- special family support needs (aging parents)
- volunteer opportunities
- family support infrastructure (churches, stores, doctors, child-care alternatives)
- special needs for special people in your family

And the list goes on and on, and every family has different needs. So while relocation complicates the negotiations process, it does not change it in any material way. During the magic time, you are creating your negotiating items short list (NISL), and issues of importance should be captured and organized into some kind of hierarchy according to importance to you as a family.

Most relocations require an iterative (back and forth) communications process at this stage. The new employer will be particularly well tuned to your reaction to the new location, and savvy employers will be focused on what is going on with the family needs as well. If your spouse has a career and will need career transition support, it will be appropriate to inquire if they provide any "trailing spouse career transition" in order to assist your mate in locating job opportunities in the new location. Outplacement firms provide this service, and your potential new employer probably has an established relationship with one or more career transition firms who compete for their business. It doesn't hurt to ask (there's that term again), and it could significantly shorten the time for your spouse to gain new employment. Hopefully this is a service that will be provided by and paid for by your new employer. If there is time during the trip, arranging a visit to the outplacement firm will provide your spouse with invaluable information about the local job market. If this is a part of the decision matrix, be sure to inquire about it before your negotiations start.

Most but not all organizations that relocate new talent have a policy on what is covered and what is not covered. Some have additional coverage for executives by exception (see appendix). You will see a vast difference if there is a regular and practiced approach to relocations. The professional association for employee relocation firms indicates that companies that do thirty or more inbound or outbound transfers annually (domestic is much different from international) tend to have a department organized to handle these issues. Below thirty (or so), these responsibilities generally fall to the HR department. Either way, understanding your needs and setting up your requirements (NISL) before you begin the negotiations process will help you immensely.

Whereas the NISL is generally a very short list, when relocation is involved, the list tends to lengthen and appropriately so. The more complicated the family unit, the longer the list, but if the employer wants you, they will be tolerant and motivated to meet your needs. Of all the nonrecurring and indirect costs of the new employee transaction, relocation costs tend to be toward the negotiable end of the scale for the precise reason that they are nonrecurring and generally handled on a individual basis, depending upon need. Internal promotions and transfers are generally handled by the same staff who handle new employee relocations, but internal transferees already have the corporate indoctrination period behind them. New employees who are going through this for the first time with an organization can't possibly ask too many questions; clarity is important. Don't be afraid to ask.

Relocation issues must be out on the table and handled before you get to any of the traditional NISL items. While it all gets rolled into one job offer and a singular new employment experience, the relocation is custom, but most other aspects of your offer will be standardized. Some will be "ERISA-fied" and totally nonnegotiable.

The Employee Retirement Income Security Act (ERISA) mandates how the communication, eligibility, and vesting of certain tax-favored (for the employer) benefits, including pensions and welfare plans, must be handled. By definition and as amended by COBRA and HIPAA, these welfare benefits must be applicable to all eligible employees in the covered class, and they cannot benefit highly compensated employees disproportionately to all other employees. These are called "qualified benefits," and there may be a whole litany of nonqualified benefits applicable to certain executive levels for which the company does not enjoy favorable tax status. Depending upon where you fit into the corporate hierarchy, some, many, or all of these might be negotiable (see appendix).

Relocation is typically not a part of the qualified benefits of a company, and while some expenses are legitimately deductible as business expenses under IRS rules, they are relatively limited, and that is why many organizations sometimes provide a gross-up of the expenses, which end up in your W-2 form at the end of the year. This gross-up of expenses, which are paid for you (directly to the IRS) by the company but are not deductible, get reported as regular and ordinary income too, so there might be a shadow effect when you get a gross-up (sometimes accompanied by a gross-up on the gross-up). As the transferring (moving) employee, you are taxed upon the expenses paid for you by the company, and this allowance is provided to lessen your tax burden. It is not automatic, but it is a negotiable item and needs to be discussed.

Negotiating all of the relo challenges allows you to get back to the basic issues of your package, and, as discussed above, the benefits side will have little negotiation room. So all of the indirect compensation like health, major medical, dental, and certain life insurance plans that are applicable to all employees in the company will not be flexible. By contrast, there is quite a lot of room to negotiate the nonqualified benefits, and the higher you go in the organization, the more negotiable this list becomes. You might not know where the lines are drawn in the sand unless you ask.

With all that has been said here about relocation, it is, at the end of the day, all peripheral to your job and what you do within that job to negotiate for your future. The primary aspects of asking for more in your base cash compensation and variable compensation and even equity (grants and stock options) will remain the same whether you are relocating across the country or just down the block. So when it comes to relocation, make certain that you explore all the variables. Clarity is important, so don't be hesitant to ask.

10

A Word or Two about the Job Search Process— You May Want to Skip This Chapter

It's complicated, it's messy, and it's done in an imperfect marketplace. It's a hurry-up-and-wait contradiction. It's exhilarating at times and crushing at times. It's the pits when you end up number two in a twenty-candidate race. As a matter of efficiency, it's better to be number twenty. It's trending in the right direction and getting more efficient ... I think. It's changing all the time. It's frustrating, and you never, ever get any feedback you can really use. In the final analysis, it's all about turning over rocks. It's always hidden under the last rock you turn over.

The "it" I am referring to is the process of getting not just any job but the perfect job. Getting hired is hard mostly, and ironically, it's sometimes easy. How you prepare matters. Who you know matters. How you research matters. How you design and execute your search matters a lot. And before it is done, you learn that you can't do it alone; your connections and your references matter too. The following chapter focuses on your references, which can make or break your candidacy. They are that important. So while this is a treatise on what to do and how to maximize the offer at the very end of the job-finding process, it could be helpful to share some things I have learned over the years about all that stuff that happens upstream before you get the offer. So if you are already at the offer stage, you can skip this chapter ... until the next time you are in the search process.

Every serious search, whether full or part-time, has three phases: a beginning, a middle, and an end phase. In the beginning phase, you must create alignment among three different realities. Before you even begin, you must adjust mentally and emotionally to the reality of your situation. Then you must align with the realities of the job search. And third, you must align the practical reality of your economic situation. These alignments are not trivial, and depending upon the circumstance that created the need to be in a job search, professional help and assistance can be very helpful and very comforting.

Once you and your mental and emotional state are in alignment for the tasks at hand, you can jump into the beginning phase, where you will need eight things:

1. A high-quality two-page resume
2. A biographical sketch
3. An accomplishments portfolio
4. A five-year base and variable income history chart
5. An exit scenario
6. References
7. An ideal job scenario
8. A strategy to obtain it

In the middle phase (which seems like it will never end, but it always does), you need to roll out your strategy and engage fully in your search, including the short-cycle, repetitive, boring, and fraught-with-rejection tasks that come with the search.

The end phase begins every time you engage your references, create your transferrable accomplishments portfolio, articulate your hundred-day plan, complete your side of the due-diligence model, and appropriately enter into negotiations upon receiving an employment offer. You may find yourself in and out of the end phase of the job search multiple times.

When done correctly, all parts line up, and a new adventure begins. The more professional help you can get in all of these phases, the shorter your search will be. Ultimately you arrive at the threshold of the negotiations process where this book can really help. In the meantime, it is a numbers game, so don't get discouraged; keep turning over rocks.

Yes, it is a numbers game. You don't get offers unless you explore opportunities. Those of us with the good fortune of working with lots of people going through the search process call it a "hit ratio." Meaning there is a relationship between how many opportunities you have to suffer through until one turns into an offer. That is your hit ratio, and some people have much better hit ratios than others. Know this: with very few exceptions, there is a job out there for everyone who really wants one ... so long as you have skills that are in demand. The demand side of the equation is constantly changing, so if you let your skills (supply side) get out of sync with real-world needs (demand side), you are in trouble. This concept is so important and so fundamental to your personal value proposition I have dedicated an entire chapter to the subject of free agency and your responsibility to keep your saw sharp ... to borrow a phrase. That would be chapter 20 at the end of the book.

This employment thing is conducted in a really large and imperfect marketplace. If you have skills that are in demand, your challenge is to find the person who needs that set of skills, and you work out a deal. That is to say, you both gain from coming to agreement. In the short run, I hope to help you achieve maximization of the economics of that agreement.

Now the old nostalgic notion of working at the same place forever, getting a pension, a silver bullet (see chapter 17), and a gold watch and enjoying your senior years rocking on a front porch somewhere is probably not going to happen for you. It wasn't likely to happen for our parents or their parents; in fact, it wasn't ever likely to happen that way. It is the great myth of Norman Rockwell Americana. Things change constantly, and we have to change with them and the other great American myth that organizations reward loyalty and commitment. That's bunk. *People* reward loyalty and commitment, not organizations. Guess what? People change too. So you have to be responsible for keeping yourself marketable—period (see chapter 20 on free agency).

According to Jack, there are only three ways for you to find your next job: reactive ways, proactive ways, and third parties. Yes, there will be some overlap in the success percentages of each, and each category varies depending on where in the economic hierarchy of the labor force you fit. Nevertheless, these three categories pretty much account for 100 percent of all jobs, so focus your search around using all three and ferret out opportunities, balancing your time among all three.

Reactive opportunities, as the name implies, are job opportunities that you see and react to. They come from postings and job sites and spider services and networking meetings that ultimately bring an opportunity to your attention. You then react to that information and make a call or send a resume, go to a job fair, answer a posting, or anything else that you choose to do in reacting to that knowledge. When it turns out to be a good match, you get a call back, which leads to an interview and perhaps a job offer. About 25 to 30 percent of all jobs are found in this manner, and this sector is growing by leaps and improves every year as the Internet and marketplace technology continue to improve. This category is very effective for lower- and midlevel jobs. The higher you are in the job and income hierarchy, the fewer the opportunities that come from this category.

Second, proactive opportunities come from your own personal networking and outreach. This category becomes more and more important as you climb the job and income spectrum. You proactively reach out through your network (in all of the various ways of reaching out), and through that human interaction, opportunities come to you that lead to an interview(s) and ultimately ... maybe, a job offer. The higher you climb, chances are that your next job opportunity will come from someone that you know or someone that they know—between 50 and 60 percent of the time.

Third-party opportunities include headhunters of all varieties. Retained search, contingency search, consulting, temp to hire, and project and independent contractor work fit in here and account for 10 to 15 percent of all jobs. At the higher levels, a disproportionate number of opportunities are funneled through retained executive search.

Your next job will emerge from one of these three areas. You should balance activities in all three categories and divide your search time according to the success percent of *your* job market represented by each. See accountability metrics below.

The actual activities you will engage in to find that next job are short-cycle, repetitive, boring, and fraught with rejection. Boy, doesn't that sound like something you really want to do every day? The short-cycle stuff is obvious, and most people learn to tolerate it, but mostly they hate it. It is the same thing over and over again a thousand times. Create your script, know your script, say your script … do it again! It's not complicated; it's just short-cycle and tedious. Ditto for the repetitive part. People find themselves wondering, *Did I just say that in this conversation or was it in the one before?* Happens all the time. Boredom sets in pretty quickly, but the routine can be mantra like. Look for the best in this process and don't let it get you down. Take frequent breaks, but measure your progress and your success as measured by the metrics below. Just when you get your hopes up for being Mr. or Ms. Right for a job, because you know you are perfect for that job … you get rejected. Rejection happens a lot. Don't take it personally; tomorrow is another day with a bunch of new rocks to turn over. Keep at it.

Adopt a routine. If someone is employed and looking for something more fulfilling, the routine will be different from the routine of someone unemployed. Usually the time available to do your search breaks down into those two camps. Your job search is either full-time or part-time depending upon your circumstances. Part-time searches usually take a lot longer, but the processes don't change. Let's talk about what a full-time search looks like, and then you can superimpose these same stages on your part-time search.

According to Jack, a full-time job search is four to six hours a day, five days a week, never on Saturday and never on Sunday … usually. If you do the math, that amounts to twenty to thirty hours per week. Do *not* think you can do ten hours on Tuesday and ten hours on Friday and accomplish anywhere near the level of productivity you get from a good solid four hours a day Monday through Friday; it can't be done. The best schedule is steady, every day, and then set it all aside when you have finished your four to six hours and go do something you consider rewarding. Reward yourself *every* day for having completed another day of short-cycle, repetitive, boring, and fraught-with-rejection stuff.

The reward doesn't matter so long as you consider it a reward. It might be as simple as a walk in the park. It might be a workout, a swim, a quiet few moments of contemplation and meditation, and perhaps some extra time with your spouse or kids. It doesn't matter as long as you consider it a reward.

A lot of full-time candidates make the mistake of working at it for ten hours a day every day, and by-golly they're gonna keep that schedule till they get that job! That experience is powerfully disturbing to the human psyche and makes you a Grinch pretty quickly. Don't do that! This is a marathon, not a sprint, and you need the stamina that short days, frequent breaks, and real rewards allow.

You will need two important administrative aids: a good calendar and a good contact manager. Technology is grand when it works, so think about backup systems for the database you will be creating. The calendar is helpful for lots of obvious reasons, including it allows you to plan your engagements, prevents double booking, provides line of sight for follow-up, and helps as a planning gadget to get the most out of your four to six hours every day. The contact manager allows you to keep track alphabetically of everyone you talk to, what was said, and what follow-up is required. But you have to put the data in. Details are important.

You also need reliable, high-speed access to the Internet and a good e-mail system, including an appropriate e-mail address. Bighunkclassof86@cox.com is not appropriate even though that has been yours since college. It won't serve you well in a job search. Don't forget to listen to your voice mail on your cell or home numbers and make certain those reflect the same attention to appropriateness as your e-mail.

You need a private, quiet place to work. You will probably be engaging in conference calls and video interviews using your computer. These are commonplace, so you need to practice with Skype and pay attention to your backdrop, ambient noise, your dress, and your expressions. Keep distractions to an absolute minimum, including children, dogs, and annoying flying insects and rotating fans. None of these mix well with video applications and screening interviews.

In addition, a reliable search engine and LinkedIn (mind your profile) are very helpful, as is social media, but be careful with your exposure and manage the information in a responsible and professional manner. Companies do access social media, and more than one candidate has been bypassed for inappropriate social media content.

I am a fan of outplacement assistance, and if you are provided this service, I suggest you take total advantage of everything offered. There are shortcuts and connections and research nuances that will take the uninitiated job seeker weeks or months, if ever, to discover without such advice and counsel. More than that, the collegiality you get from the networking and the solid counsel of a caring human being in a coaching relationship is highly beneficial. I admit that I am biased on this subject. You can purchase similar services from "retail" providers of these services but be very cautious and exercise great care to know exactly what you are getting for your hard-earned money.

There are also many employment-networking services that are totally free or very low cost to attend. Check your local newspaper or business journal for the schedule of networking meetings. By all means go. Practice talking about yourself. It's hard but gets easier. Self-aggrandizement is not comfortable for anyone, and that is exactly what it feels like, but you will have to get accustomed to talking about you, your accomplishments, and how you can add value.

Whether you are part-time or full-time in your search, you need all these things and more. You'll also need a method of evaluating your effectiveness to keep you on track. I have advised job seekers for over twenty years, and I have distilled three metrics that are leading indicators of how well you are doing. Remember— this job search thing is a process. It has a beginning, a middle (that seems never ending), and an end phase. Every job search ends in a celebration as you go on to what comes next. Don't forget to celebrate.

I call them accountability metrics. There are only three you want to track and evaluate:

(1) How many hours did you spend in your job search this week? Be honest.

Evaluate total time against the four to six hours per day, five days a week, which equals twenty to thirty hours target. Balance your search time between_reactive, proactive, and third parties and don't spend a higher percentage of your time than the success percentages mentioned above.

(2) How many "touches" did you have this week? A touch is a two-way communication with another human being in the context of performing your search. Evaluate against prior week numbers in an effort to grow to your ideal number.

(3) How many "opportunities" did you pursue this week? An opportunity is a real job that you applied for by sending in your resume and cover letter. Evaluate against prior week application numbers and seek to grow. There is no such thing as too many applications filed.

This evaluation is for you; you need to be satisfied with the outcome of these three metrics. As you do better in each of these three areas of your search, you will find your search activities becoming more efficient. Notice the absence of "number of interviews conducted" as a metric of importance. Interviews are a derivative of doing the basics of the search process. If you mind those three metrics and work hard to improve them toward the ideal every week, the interviews will come. As interviews come, so will offers. Offers lead to negotiations and (you guessed it) the opportunity to ask for more.

CHAPTER 11

Drafting Your References

I purposely mentioned references only in passing in the previous chapter, but I attribute much of your job-finding success or failure as a candidate to how your references deliver when you need them. Throughout your career, you will need references who speak well of you and are very comfortable recommending you for hire. If you are midcareer or senior in your career, there is an emergence of a second shadow reflection called your reputation. There should be a consistency if not a symmetry between your reputation and your references. Your reputation is not just behind you; it envelops you and occasionally even precedes you like an aura. Your reputation is a real thing, and it exists whether you like it or not. Changing an established reputation can be difficult. The beliefs and opinions that form your reputation are what they are and can't be carefully selected like your references. Reputations can be sullied much faster than it takes to build a good one, so always guard your reputation carefully.

You are in charge of your references, and they must be selected and groomed carefully. You are not in charge of your reputation except in the sense that you get what you deserve. These two concepts adopt a parallel path throughout your productive years, each separate but (hopefully) never far from one other.

You can reach out and talk to your references and appreciate and inform and "program" them to a certain extent. Reputations are intangible, ephemeral, and a bit in the wind. Reputations are like the wake behind your boat, something that marks your passing, but when you stop or slow down, it encircles you and gets out in front of you and frequently even precedes you. Sometimes it is a good thing, sometimes not. You need to be consciously aware of your reputation, and you need to attend to it. Your reputation is much like a legacy, and your references are more like your PR reps.

What I call "drafting your references" is a four-stage process that requires them to pay close attention to detail and learn all about you. It is helpful if they are agreeable to a certain programming process, which includes an automatic debrief call back to you when they have done their duty as your reference. This sounds complicated, and it is, but when done correctly, it will serve you well at a critical stage in the due diligence process. Keep in mind that these stages are spread out over your entire search time, so it looks like a lot more work than it is. If you really care about what your PR reps say about you, and you should, you'll follow this formula closely. It pays off.

Stage One: Selection
Stage Two: Draft, Prepare, and Put on Ice
Stage Three: Thaw, Program
Stage Four: Automate the Feedback

Here's a one-paragraph summary of what these four stages might look like during an actual search:

You start with selecting the right people; you must choose carefully. You then move on to draft, prepare, and ice. Sounds like a party, but drafting is all about asking them be a reference, gaining acceptance, preparing them with just the right information, explaining how it will work, and then putting them on "ice" until needed. Then, as you do your search, you'll want to regularly update them on your progress. Later, when you get a request for references (always a very good sign), ask the potential employer what kind of references they would like. Most will choose categories of people, such as boss, peer, subordinate, and client-customer, but let them tell you what categories they want. Since you have already drafted your references by category, you are way ahead of the game. Let the prospective employer know that you will return this list in twenty-four hours. Now you call them up, thaw them out, manage their expectations, and program them why you are "perfect" for the job. Then program them to make a follow-up call to debrief you. Muy importante!

Let's Start with Stage One: Selection

References are people chosen for a task because you are 97.636 percent certain they will support you enthusiastically. If you have any doubt about a reference, don't use them. Select only platinum-plated people that will pander to your near perfect professionalism. No one else will do!

Everything starts with your selection of who gets to officially talk about you. I have recommended for some time now that you follow the 360-degree rule of twos (360 x 2): Two bosses, two peers, two subordinates (if you have them), and two client-customers. The reason I recommend this 360-degree selection of references is because, in a sparkling display of observational subtlety, that is what most organizations (and headhunters) ask for.

A recent survey of applicant tracking systems revealed slightly less than half request references as part of the original application. Some won't let you leave them blank and require the field to be completed before you can submit the application. Do *not* put your references on these forms because you lose control of your references that way. This is entirely too soon to be revealing information that is generally reserved for the due diligence stage. If the applicant tracking system (ATS) system insists, then insert Mickey Mouse, Santa Claus, and the Tooth Fairy, each with their own imaginary phone number and see if that doesn't meet their needs. If you lose control of your references, there is no way for this system to work for you.

Once upon a time, employers also asked for personal references, and occasionally they still do, but the value proposition of personal references has questionable job relatedness in the hiring process, and most employers have ceased this practice. What is much more relevant for the hiring manager and company is how you engage, manage, support, reward, develop, sustain, respect, deliver to, respond to, strategize with, argue with, probe, jest, question, train, and develop these bosses, peers, subordinates, and customers. That knowledge is job relevant and transferrable to the new employer in realistic and meaningful ways.

In reverse order, begin with customer-clients. Anyone who is downstream from your work is a customer. While a customer can be someone who bought something from you, it does not have to be. Customer is more important as a relationship statement. A customer can be any person that has received your work product in a downstream professional relationship. Customers can be internal or external to your company, depending upon your career path. Customers are important and relevant to the due diligence stage because of the uniqueness of being on the receiving end of what you do—in particular, what you did when things went wrong.

Subordinates are those who have reported to you in the organizational sense. If you are applying for a supervisory job, this set of references will be mission critical to your success, so choose them carefully. Bad bosses populate all levels of the job market, and some are in the job market *because* they are bad bosses. Hiring companies don't want to make the mistake of hiring a bad manager/supervisor, and they will check these references closely. And then they might even ask these references for other references who worked with them. Secondary reference checking has become a common practice, particularly among the professional reference-checking set. It is also one way of hunting for your reputation. Subordinates are important and relevant to the due diligence stage because supervisors are agents of management, and the employer is vicariously liable for their misbehavior. More importantly, survey after survey among American companies indicates that turnover is caused by bad bosses more than any other reason. So you might want to cover this secondary reference inquiry with your chosen references. I will make a suggestion about this in the programming paragraph later in this section.

Peers, no surprise, are the ladies and gentlemen you worked with who are on the same (approximate) organizational level as you. Peers do not have to be in your same department, but, generally speaking, the most relevant peer relationships will be. Also important for consideration will be peers in other functional organizations with whom your function has close and perhaps dependent relationship. These peer relationships are important and relevant to the due diligence stage because they identify your ways of influencing organizational outcomes over which you have no real line authority.

Lastly and most importantly is the boss relationship. By the way, previous employer boss relationships are fine unless the hiring company specifically has instructed you otherwise. Bosses are special and will get a special line of questioning. It is not unusual for your new boss to want to check these references rather than having HR or a contractor do it. Most all of us manage "up" slightly different from how we manage all other relationships. While only a few jobs actually work at the pleasure of the boss, almost all of us tend to treat the boss relationship as special. Interestingly, most bosses realize that, but surprisingly few actually know how their subordinates adjust their style and demeanor, and fewer still are capable of articulating those differences. Most think what they see is what actually is, and nothing could be further from the truth. A certain amount of upward deference is appropriate but not so much that it masks the real person, and if there is a lot of it going on, the peers, subordinates, and customers will know about it. The boss relationship is important and relevant to the due diligence phase because the elasticity of give and take at the boss level cannot be ambiguous, and if you are going to get the offer, this relationship is the gateway to it and to your future success as well. After you have selected eight such individuals (two in each category), we ask them to serve.

Stage Two: Draft, Prepare, and Put on Ice

Draft in this context means reach out and ask each of your selections from stage one to actually serve as your reference. Most people are flattered and a little bit apprehensive, but if you have chosen right, you can cancel that feeling right away. Explain that you are in a full-scale job search (if applicable; if it is a low-key and confidential, it still works the same) and because of your previous relationship with them, you would like them to consider being a reference provider when the time comes. Prep them with your new resume and bio or whatever marketing materials you have developed so they can refresh their knowledge of the total you. There is nothing quite so bad as an uninformed reference. We guard against that by preparing them with the resume in advance (and again later if necessary); you let them know that before anyone calls them, you will alert them about the call with at least a day's notice. You can do this easily if you stick to the formula. You also ask that they call you with feedback whenever anyone contacts them for a reference. This is an important step that should be very natural for them.

References are generally comforted by knowing that you will call them in advance to prepare them for the inquiry. By the way, that is just common courtesy. Think about it. If you have ever received a call out of the blue from a potential employer of a friend, colleague, subordinate, or (heaven forbid) boss, indicating that you were given as a reference, you probably felt totally unprepared and maybe a little miffed about that call, as it put you in an awkward place. Well, this formula does not allow that to happen.

You close this conversation with your reference, each individually ... all eight of them, by assuring them that you will be back in touch with them in advance of anyone calling. They will appreciate that. The added side benefit, and this happens all the time, is that you are now occupying a special place in their mind. You have just signed up another member of your job search posse, and if any fitting and appropriate job crosses their path, you are going to hear about the opportunity—and quickly. Remember—most people find it flattering to be asked to provide a reference. It is a position of trust and esteem, and it has an elevating impact on your relationship, and they want to serve you well.

Follow up with a letter to them (e-mail is fine) recognizing and appreciating their newly adopted role. Include your marketing materials (resume and bio) and reiterate that you will call in advance of anyone calling them. That effectively puts them on "ice," and you are now done with stage two.

Meanwhile, the Search Gets Underway

Between stage two and stage three, you get busy with your search. Your references are on ice, and you have been doggedly turning over rocks in pursuit of that next job. Sooner or later (hopefully sooner), you are going to arrive at the due diligence stage. The company likes you and wants to take it all to the next level.

Generally, arriving at the due diligence stage of the employment process is an indication that you have made it to the short list. This means that all the riffraff has been sorted through, and the decision makers have narrowed the field. Intense scrutiny now begins. Hiring companies don't waste expensive resources checking references until the field has narrowed. So you get the call that goes something like this: "Hello, Greg, the hiring committee here at Acme Tool would like to let you know we are inviting you back for a (second, third, fourth) round of interviews, and we are hopeful of making a hiring decision within the very near future. As a preparatory measure for this stage, we would like to contact your references and get a feel for what it is like working with you. Would you be able to supply us with some references?"

At this point, you gesture a celebratory "Yes!" and you say, "Sure! What kind of references would you like?" Let them tell you what they want. They will most likely request bosses, peers, subordinates, and customers or some close variation. And then you say, "Sure, can you give me a day to come up with those, and I'll send you the names and contact information?" It might also be appropriate to ask who will be doing the reference checking. More and more now, organizations are outsourcing the reference-checking process, and it would be helpful for you to know this so you can prepare your PR posse accordingly.

This is how you always get the time necessary to call your PR reps and let them know in advance who is going to call and when. Enter stage three.

Stage Three: Thaw and Program

Armed with the information of who is going to call and when, you place a call to each of your chosen references, as promised, and alert them. They will appreciate your call and will immediately start wondering where they put your resume and bio information. Take them off the hook and offer to send an updated version. If there has been a passage of time between ice and thaw, you will probably have changed or customized your resume a couple of times, so updating the reference with your new information is a wise move.

Then, after explaining when and who is going to call, let your reference know about the job title and the scope of the position, and then *carefully explain why you are perfect for this job*. Use those words. "Mike, let me tell you why I think I'm perfect for this job ..." Limit your perfection to one or two short sentences. Complex notions get lost, so keep it simple. Find a way to repeat it at least one more time during the phone call. You have hit a home run if, by chance, they spontaneously play back to you why you are "perfect" during the call. Close by expressing your appreciation for their effort and remind them when it is over you would like a call from them to debrief. Set this up so that they automatically call you after they have given a reference and while it is fresh in their mind.

This is what I mean when I say "program" your references. If you find repetitive ways of emphasizing why you think you are perfect for the job, guess what? They will do the same at some point in their conversation with the reference checker. They will predictably find a way to weave your perfection into their conversation. If you have chosen your specific perfections wisely, this is worth its weight in gold.

Now, therein lies the challenge, selecting and simplifying one or two (at the most) attributes or experiences or competencies that you possess and know the hiring organization needs. Finding and articulating the right things to prepare your reference is worth some careful thinking and planning.

The subject of preparing your references for the potential inquiry about "who else" the reference checker might speak with (someone else who worked with you at the same time and place, for example) may be stretching the limits of what you can expect from a volunteer PR rep. Nevertheless, you should think about it because the trend now is to use more third-party specialists to check references, and this technique is frequently used by outsourced firms. Should you choose to do so, this detail may pay off big time. So brainstorming with your reference about whom they might suggest if asked can be contingency planning time well spent. If you determine that your potential employer is planning to use a third-party outsourced professional reference firm, the possibility doubles that this technique will be used.

After you have made all your programming calls, create the e-mail back to the company with the references, relationships, and contact information and make certain that you seize the moment to add "as promised, here are your (six, seven, or eight) references with contact information." The twenty-four hours you requested to come up with the references was actually the time you used to program your references who were on ice, waiting to be helpful in your job search.

Stage Four: Automate the Feedback

Prompt follow-up is most beneficial. During your programming call, you requested that your reference give you a post-reference call debrief as soon as they can. Getting this feedback is important information for you to help manage your search. Getting the debrief calls also keeps you in the loop about the company's progress in contacting your references. Among the issues you would like to know from the debrief are the following: who contacted them and when, how long the conversation was, what primary questions were asked, the general assessment your reference had about the call. Did he/she get into any detail on competencies, skills, or attributes needed for the job? Was there any secondary reference request, and if so, whom did they suggest? This will let you know if your programming paid off.

As you get the debrief calls from your references, you will be able to discern any emerging patterns or drill-down questions that might forecast some specific concerns being examined during the reference checks, the absence of which is encouraging.

So while it sounds a little daunting, this level of detail about managing your references will pay off for you in tangible ways because hardly anyone does this. Very few professionals go through this much trouble to prepare their references, but references can make or break your candidacy.

CHAPTER 12

Headhunters

Headhunters is a much-abused term used to describe all sorts of business and service firms that supply talent to employers for a fee. Who pays that fee varies. Mostly companies pay, but depending upon the structure, employees or candidates can also wind up paying a fee. Even worse, in some conditions, hopeful candidates can pay a fee where no job emerges at all. The vast majority of employment services firms and "personnel agencies," as some are still known, are run by hardworking and sincere people who get a great deal of personal and professional pride out of helping other people find work. A few are unscrupulous bloodsuckers that thrive on deception, and that minority tarnishes the industry for all. If you are in a job search and someone wants in your wallet, run away; don't walk.

Headhunters are responsible for approximately 12 to 20 percent of all jobs. If you include the temporary industry in all of its variations of temp-only, temp-to-perm (this is a real misnomer—there are no permanent jobs), independent contractor relationships, and special-project assignments, you might get close to 22 maybe 23 percent of the labor force at any given moment. It's safe to say the industry is responsible for millions and millions of jobs, and every job seeker should be active in this (headhunter) category.

Certain slices of the labor market are dominated, if not controlled, by project-based temporary employment (staffing) companies. High-tech and high-paying jobs are figuring large in this new trend. The US Bureau of Labor Statistics reports that the US Temporary Help Penetration Rate—the percentage of total jobs held by temporary employees—hit an all-time high of 2.04 percent of the labor force in June 2015. While that may not sound very large, it represents 2.9 million workers, up 70 percent from 1995, when the penetration rate was 1.48 percent and the total US workforce was about 20 percent smaller. [#12]

Several large European economies, including the UK, Germany, and France, currently have temporary job penetration rates above 2 percent. In the UK, the rate is almost 4 percent [#13] and climbing back toward its prior peak of 4.6 percent before the 2008–2009 global recession. Regulatory burdens in the United States, such as the Affordable Care Act, have increased the cost of carrying full-time employees, with the result that the United States is looking more like Europe as far as temporary/contract employment is concerned. This fuels demand for temporary staffing solutions in the United States, and it is a growth sector.

Importantly, the term headhunter also applies to the retained search and the contingency search businesses, and their placement rates are included in the 20 to 23 percent figures mentioned above. Suffice to say this is a huge influence on the job market, the employment process, *and* the negotiations landscape where headhunters are involved.

Let's spend a few minutes making sure that we are clear on the job search categories and the success rates for each that I mentioned in detail in chapter 10. While there is certainly overlap in the categories of successful ways that people find jobs, I recommended for years that candidates divide their search time up in 60/30/10 percent categories. By that I mean (see again chapter 10) a full-time job search is best completed working Monday through Friday, four to six hours a day, totaling twenty to thirty hours per week—no more. Sixty percent of most professional employment is found in the proactive category, which is driven primarily by the candidate's personal and professional network. Half that many jobs (30 percent but growing rapidly) were found through the reactive category, which is driven by the Internet, job postings, and data collectors like spider sites. Finally, 10 percent of their time, more or less, should be spent exploiting the headhunter community. So as the recession recedes and the great middle-class numbers begin to swell again, the mix of those numbers (60, 30, 10) may shift a bit, but my point is you cannot do a complete and thorough search without spending some time working with the headhunter industry.

There is an interesting phenomenon going on within the search industry, particularly among the retained search sector. That is, there exists an inverse relationship between the slice of the market figures represented by retained search. A greater and growing percentage of the higher compensated professional jobs are represented by retained search. Now the triangle of available highly compensated jobs narrows toward the top, and retained search represents over half of all these jobs over $250,000 in annual compensation.

According to a 2014 scholarly research paper by Peter Cappelli [#14] (Wharton School, University of Pennsylvania) and Monika Hamori (Instituto Empresa, Madrid, Spain) from 2001 to 2003, large employers in the United States used executive search firms to fill 54 percent of jobs paying above $250,000 (source: International Assn. of Corporate Professional Recruiters, 2003). Many of the remaining vacancies would have been filled through internal promotion, which suggests that the percentage of outside hiring that does not use executive search firms may be quite small. Retained search (in which the search firm works under an exclusive contract with the client and is paid a fee even if no hire is made) has become a fixture in the labor market for executives and other highly skilled workers, with companies spending an estimated $10.4 billion in search fees [#15] in 2011 alone (source: Assoc. of Executive Search Consultants).

By the way, the big five in the executive search business are Korn/Ferry International, Egon Zehnder International, Spencer Stuart, Heidrick & Struggles, and Russell Reynolds Associates, just in case you are considering a change at the senior level.

Contingency search firms, by comparison, are paid by the employer contingent on the person hired being referred by that firm. The single most important difference between retained and contingent search is client control. Retained search has absolute control of who gets through their screening process, and the contingent side of the business has no such control. So one of the things you always want to know when approached by a headhunter is if the search is retained or contingency. The answer is important to you because of this control issue.

Either way, when a headhunter is involved in the recruiting process, knowing the relationship with the client is important. Either way, you should not be paying the bill, but you must always look to how the money flows to determine where the client loyalties lay. While a close, communicative relationship with the headhunter is helpful, remember that they do *not* represent you. Retained search professionals are very adept at gaining your confidence, and like a heat-seeking missile, they go straight for the heart of the matter and do their very best to make certain that there are *no* negotiations and the offer as given from the employer will be accepted. Remain cautious about how much you share and how much you disclose about your financial expectations because one of their duties is to help the company with this confidential insider information that assures the ultimate employment offer will be accepted. Headhunters do this by establishing a trust-based relationship with you and discussing your needs and wants, and they share *all* of that with the employer. At some point, the headhunter is going to be asked by the employer what the offer must be in order to gain acceptance from the candidate. The headhunter's credibility rests on their ability to answer that question with certainty.

Occasionally, the headhunter is empowered to actually extend the employment offer in the name of the company. You do not want to be negotiating with anyone who has no real authority. You must make it clear that you need the offer in writing and from the employer ... no middlemen allowed. Be careful and use great finesse, but the headhunter is not the one paying your salary, so make certain that you are actually negotiating with your employer, not a third party. Do your best to discuss the terms and conditions directly with your new supervisor or a responsible professional in the HR department.

CHAPTER 13

Culture and Fit Still Matter

Know what the root word of "culture" is? *Cult.* Suddenly it starts to sound ominous, but in the organizational sense, it isn't ominous, it isn't tangible, and you can't see it—but it's real, and it's powerful, and it surrounds every organization like a cloud that doesn't go away. Culture in the organizational sense translates to "how we do things here," and every organization has at least one descriptively dominant culture, sometimes more than one. Almost always the culture is created by the shadow of the leader, and true leaders are sensitive to any differences between the real and the perceived cultures in their companies.

Recently, Jeff Bezos, founder and leader of Amazon, Blue Origin and the Washington Post found himself embroiled in a culture clash between his perception of the culture at Amazon and the perception of over a hundred current and previous employees who were interviewed for an article in the *New York Times* [#16]. The *Miami Herald* picked up the story, and before Mr. Bezos could blink, there was a viral culture bash going on. Technology companies populate the front wave of social media, and those little electrons travel at the speed of light. The *Times* piece recounted numerous episodes of nonsympathetic managers and graphic, firsthand accounts about the notion of big brother and big data working together to monitor the productivity of employees, and once the genie was out of the bottle, it got stretched all out of proportion. At my publisher's deadline, the battle was waning and a recent cover story for Fortune indicated the storm may have calmed. Bezos has a lot of employees, and it is highly likely that he has little daily involvement in culture management, but his response was refined and immediate, and clearly culture matters to Mr. Bezos—and he said so with a quick and decisive communications blitz to all of his employees with a personal appeal. Good first step, Mr. B. Stay on it; manage it. It's important; your corporate culture and reputation are at stake here!

Like I said, all organizations have a culture, and the implications of both good and bad cultures will emerge in the bottom-line performance of the organization. Companies with positive cultures tend to thrive, while the opposite is true of companies with poor cultures. Leadership must take an active role in defining how things are done "around here." Assessing the culture of a potential new employer requires a bit of social media sleuthing, but thanks to the Internet and a number of transparency websites, you can get the lowdown pretty quickly. Among them, try www. Glassdoor.com, who in less than ten years has come on the scene and has collected over eight million reviews of more than 400,000 employers. Try a literature search that keys off the name of the employer for newspapers, magazines, and most other print media. Don't forget the power of pure old-fashioned networking. LinkedIn can be one of your best research tools for checking out the real culture from folks who work there now or did so in their past. Very nifty, this sleepy little thing called LinkedIn. There are even specialty companies betting their very existence on the demand for measurement metrics of company culture, and all indications are that this will be a big business in the future.

One of the icons of the human capital side of the enterprise, Ann Rhoades recently completed a book on the importance of culture and values in the success of the enterprise. Ann is PRES (person responsible for exceptional service) of People Ink, an HR consulting firm she founded that guides companies to define and develop cultural environments that support corporate goals. Her book is *Built on Values,* cowritten with Nancy Shepherdson [#17].

Ann, before starting her own consulting firm and before becoming one of the founders of Jet Blue Airlines, was chief people officer at Southwest Airlines, and she reported directly to the legendary Herb Kelleher (speaking of corporate culture). One of her most poignant Herb Kelleher quotes is "Culture is what happens when no one is looking." You don't have to dig very deep to uncover a lot of information about the culture at Southwest Airlines, but unless Southwest is your new employer, you will need specific ways of evaluating the values fit between you, the employer, and your new boss.

According to Rhoades, leaders drive values, values drive behavior, behaviors drive culture, and cultures drive performance. This resonates with everything I believe from just about forty years in the HR business.

As a candidate for employment, it is important for you to realize that you can't see values ... but you can see behavior, and the actual behavior of the leaders must be consistent with the values they espouse. If not, the credibility of the organization suffers, and a values crisis emerges. Even more importantly, there needs to be an appropriate fit between you and your new company and the manager you will report to and how things are done.

Jack Zenger and Joseph Folkman, both PhD-level cofounders of their own consulting company in Utah and frequent contributors to the *Harvard Business Review*, published an article in 2013 [#18] that questioned, *what's the one factor that most affects how satisfied, engaged, and committed you are at work?* All of their research over the years points to one answer: your immediate supervisor.

Zenger and Folkman went on to say, quite simply, the better the leader, the more engaged the staff. Take, for example, results from a recent study they did on the effectiveness of 2,865 leaders in a large financial-services company. They observe that you can see a straight-line correlation between levels of employee engagement and the measure of the overall effectiveness of their supervisors, as judged not just by the employees themselves but by their bosses, colleagues, and other associates on 360 assessments. At the low end, the satisfaction, engagement, and commitment levels of employees toiling under the worst leaders (below the tenth percentile) reached only the fourth percentile. (That means 96 percent of the company's employees were more satisfied/ engaged/committed.) At the other end, the best leaders (those in the ninetieth percentile) were supervising the happiest, most engaged, most committed employees—those happier than more than 92 percent of their colleagues. [#19]

They note that this study is by no means unusual. They saw the same pattern in the United States, the UK, the Netherlands, Spain, United Arab Emirates, and India. It is common to financial services, manufacturing, high-tech, government, universities, hospitals, food services, energy, and every other industry they studied. They saw it in organizations employing 225,000 people and 250 people.

Zenger and Folkman conclude that this matters for two very basic reasons. *First, bad bosses negate other investments.* None of the expensive programs a company institutes to increase employee engagement—excellent rewards, well-thought-out career paths, stimulating work environments, EAP programs, health insurance, and all other perks combined—will make much difference to the people stuck with bad bosses. *Second, good bosses lead employees to increase revenue.* And, as many other studies have shown, there's a strong correlation between employee engagement, customer satisfaction, and healthy corporate revenue generation.

Now, the same is true for you. You have your own personal set of values, and these values drive your behavior, so you need to identify whether or not your brand of values matches well with the organization and with your soon-to-be immediate supervisor. You need to be crystal clear about what is important to you in the workplace.

You also need a method of ascertaining the potential employer's values *before* you get to the offer stage. No amount of negotiating in any channel will bring these together if they are divergent from your own. It is best to learn it as part of the discovery process while you are interviewing and cut your losses if they don't match. Social media can help, research can help, and pure networking can help.

On both sides of this ledger, yours and the company's, it is called "fit." How you fit the organizational culture is a matter of how your values line up with the values of the organization. One thing is for certain; you do not want to be explaining that the fit was not right twelve to fifteen months down the road to another employer. This is important. If you end up discovering that your values don't mesh with your employer's values or vice versa, the outcome will be the same. It means constant conflict and suboptimized performance, and you will find yourself right back in the job search again.

One of the often overlooked but generally available indicators of corporate values is, of course, what the employer says about this subject in their literature and on their website. Start with a thorough examination of the company materials. If supporting your community is important to you, see if you can find out what exactly the company does to be a good corporate neighbor and what, if any, philanthropy the organization supports. The nexus between the company and the community is an important part of most corporate brands, and that brand transfers directly to you once you start working for an organization. Take the time to investigate and don't forget to ask.

CHAPTER
14

Gender Differences

Please remember that at the onset I let you know this is not a scientific, fact-based, statistically laden book filled with data to support my hypothesis about negotiations. It is an experiential book based upon my personal interactions over decades of working with men and women seeking employment. Intuitively, I felt that women are at a general disadvantage in negotiations, and by extension, salary negotiations specifically, primarily because they don't ask. By the way, that is not all that earthshaking; most people don't ask, men and women. But my feeling was that women didn't ask at a far greater rate than men. I just don't have empirical data to back that up. Not to worry—significant work has been done on this subject, and by far greater researchers than me.

In my own personal experience discussing this assessment with hundreds of female executives, I have found them to be in general agreement that women don't ask. Why? Well that's complicated. My own personal experience is highly subjective and anecdotal and revolves around a general reluctance women have to ask for more. Many of the women I have worked with want to be recognized for their hard work and accomplishments and paid a competitive rate on the basis of their value and contribution to the organization. This requires a great amount of faith that there is an invisible hand somewhere in the organization that functions as the great arbiter of fairness and virtue that will swoop in and drop buckets of rewards, money, recognition, promotions, and so forth on only the deserving and ignore the requests and demands of others less worthy. Worthy, admirable, wholesome....but, very lacking in realism.

Many of the women I have worked with in career transition, when asked to tell their stories of negotiations, have simply said that was not their style. They preferred to accept an appropriate offer, get into the job, and demonstrate their competency and value, hopeful that those contributions would in return be noticed, valued, and rewarded. That belief alone leaves them approaching the starting gate in the race with their male counterparts who are already rounding the first turn. Men generally think and act differently.

This whole complex of insecurity, uncertainty, sensitivity, and reluctance results in most women taking a very passive approach to negotiating for themselves. Not infrequently, a female executive who normally has a hard-as-nails approach to negotiations as part of her job will simply defer in the context of personal salary negotiations for herself. Most men don't understand that, don't get it, and don't even think about any of that. To the contrary, most men have been raised to believe that they can change the world they live in, and most women have been raised to believe they must accept the world they live in. In the process, they leave honey pots full of money sitting in their employer treasury.

In the abundant literature on negotiations, there is little on the subject of gender differences. But the definitive study, if proof of an empirical nature is necessary, is a slightly dated book by Linda Babcock and Sara Laschever that goes by the title *Women Don't Ask ... Negotiation and the Gender Divide,* [20] published by Princeton. Their more recent follow-up work, *Ask for It,* is [21] equally compelling and expands upon their initial concepts and brings to light four new ones. Both are great reads, done in a disciplined manner and backed by not only multiple true-life examples but also scientific research with sufficient statistical rigor to assuage even the most skeptical nonbelievers. In doing this, they create an extraordinary mosaic of a complicated answer to a complicated question. I recommend both books to both genders of all ages as an enlightening experience to illuminate the many vagaries of gender differences in negotiations.

My experience reading their books was a confirmation, beyond any doubt, that my nonscience-based intuitive model was correct but seriously lacking when it comes to causality, and these two authors spend a great deal of energy pointing out exactly why such gender differences exist.

Another recent work that is worth your time if you are seriously interested in this subject (after all, you're reading this) is *Lean In* by Sheryl Sandberg and Nell Scovell, [#22] published by Knopf in 2013. It's recent, it's hip (unlike Make More Money), and it's remarkably parallel to the same complicated causal factors that Babcock and Laschever unveiled in their work. Sandberg is a rocket-to-the-top female executive and a classic example of how it can be done in the male-dominated world we currently live in. It needs to be said that she is scary smart and by most reports somehow remains a friendly, approachable, "real person" who has not been spoiled by it all. She also possesses an uncanny power of observation and the intellectual ability to connect the dots and find solutions in this uncertain business world. The essence of the book is in its title; she saw too many capable women leaning out as opposed to sitting at the table leaning in.

Lean In is a book for professional women to help them achieve their career goals and for men who want to contribute to a more equitable society. The book looks at the barriers preventing women from taking leadership roles in the workplace, barriers such as discrimination, blatant and subtle sexism, and sexual harassment. She also examines societal barriers, such as the fact that women still work the double day and the devaluing of work inside the home as opposed to work outside the home. Along with the latter, there are the barriers that women create for themselves through internalizing systematic discrimination and societal-based gender roles. Sandberg argues that in order for change to happen, women need to break down these societal and personal barriers by striving for, accepting, and succeeding at leadership roles. The ultimate goal is to encourage women to lean in to positions of leadership because she asserts that by having more female voices in positions of power, there will be more equitable opportunities created for everyone.

According to Sandberg, "A truly equal world would be one where women ran half our countries and companies and men ran half our homes." How is that for a thoughtful, poignant, provocative suggestion?

Sandberg lost her husband and father of their two young children in an uncanny accident in May 2015 while the family was on vacation in Mexico. I share the global sentiment that this tragic loss does not, in the long run, diminish her beacon of leadership and example for all women around the world of how to do it all. She is going to do something truly special in this world.

Both of these two works put the microscope on female performance and ask the question, why are things the way they are? Giving substance and credibility to my intuitive belief that women don't ask in greater numbers than men and why they don't are two seminal outcomes of the research and writing done by Babcock and Laschever. As they observe, "Asking for what you want is the essential first step that 'kicks-off' a negotiation. If you miss your chance to negotiate, the best negotiation advice in the world isn't going to help you much. And women simply aren't 'asking' at the same rate as men."

The first issue of importance has to do with psychological work done by Julian Rotter, dating from 1954. Rotter was an American psychologist known for developing influential theories, including social learning theory as well as this notion of locus of control. He was a faculty member at the Ohio State University and then the University of Connecticut. A *Review of General Psychology* survey, published in 2002, ranked Rotter as the sixty-fourth most cited psychologist of the twentieth century.

According to Rotter, locus of control [#23] refers to the extent to which individuals believe they can control events affecting them. A person's locus is either internal (low scores) where the person believes they can control their life or external (high scores), meaning they believe their decisions and life are controlled by environmental factors that they cannot influence.

Individuals with a strong internal locus of control believe events in their life derive primarily from their own actions. For example, when receiving exam results, people with an internal locus of control tend to praise or blame themselves and their abilities. People with a strong external locus of control tend to praise or blame external factors, such as the teacher or the exam.

According to Babcock and Laschever, the average scores for women are significantly higher on the locus of control scales than those for men, meaning that women are more likely to believe that their circumstances are controlled by others while men are more likely to believe that they can influence their circumstances and opportunities through their own actions. And, they go on, it is not just true for American women. A 1997 study by Peter B. Smith, Shaun Dugan, and Fons Trompenaars (1996) published [#24] in the *Journal of Cross-Cultural Psychology* confirmed this same finding in fourteen countries, including Great Britain, Belgium, the Netherlands, and Sweden in Western Europe; Bulgaria, Czechoslovakia, Hungary, Poland, and Romania in Eastern Europe; the former USSR, India, China, Mexico, and Brazil.

The first phenomenon for women to confront is locus of control (LOC) scores that indicate that women, when compared to men, don't have anywhere close to the sense that they are as much in control of their world as men do.

The second issue is a collection of causes all enabled and facilitated by the LOC problem just mentioned. According to Babcock and Lashover, women frequently feel unsure about what they deserve, worry that asking for too much may threaten a relationship, or fear that the people around them will react badly if they ask for too much. Women are also less optimistic than men about what they can get from a negotiation, they feel less comfortable than men with risk taking, and they frequently lack confidence in their negotiating ability, resulting in asking only for things that will be easy to get.

There is a well-developed theme in their book about the societal influences that create "gender schema," which is defined as basically all the programming that goes into making boys into men and girls into women, which creates the daily reality of this syndrome as a product of the grand alchemy of self-limiting influences that are part of the feminine mystique today.

One of their most poignant examples results from a study by economist Sara Solnick, who created what she called the "Ultimatum Game" to observe the general attitudes toward men and women when they are negotiating. In this game, the researchers give two people ten dollars to divide amongst themselves. One person, the "proposer," suggests a division of the money between the two players, like "Six dollars for me and four dollars for you." The other player, the "responder," decides whether to accept the offer or not. If the responder accepts, the two players are paid the suggested amounts. If the responder rejects the offer, both players get nothing and the game is over. No discussion, no dialogue, no back and forth ... just acceptance or rejection, as in ultimatum. The players know the rules in advance, and it is one shot only!

Supposedly, the game helps researchers understand people's perceptions of fairness and how these perceptions influence their behavior. If fairness were not an issue, self-interest would motivate most proposers to suggest $9.99 for themselves and $.01 for the responder. However, once fairness is factored in, each proposer must guess at the minimum amount the responder will accept as fair. The responder must then decide whether the offer is fair enough to be acceptable or so unfair that getting nothing is preferable.

To research how notions of gender influence behavior, Solnick informed the players only about the gender of their colleague, and the exchange was done through a blind they never actually met. After multiple iterations of the ultimatum game, mixing roles and genders multiple times, Solnick discovered two interesting things. First, she found that both men and women made less generous offers to female responders than to male responders, 12 percent lower on average. This outcome argues that players of both sexes expect women to accept less than men. Solnick's second finding turned out to be the flip side of the first: both male and female responders required much larger offers from women than they required from men to make an offer acceptable, a stunning 42.5

percent larger. We don't just insist that women accept less, Solnick discovered; we also demand that women give away more.

Just in case you are not yet convinced, the expectation that women will demand less and accept less and give away more is also demonstrated by other research by Babcock and Laschever. Only 16 percent of the hundreds interviewed by the authors for their book said that they think women make better negotiators than men. Because beliefs can be such powerful determinants of behavior, when translated into practice, this belief will lead many people, if not most, to expect that they'll be able to reach better agreements (from their point of view) when they're negotiating with women than with men. This expectation, according to Babcock and Laschever, consciously or subconsciously will lead them to set higher targets against women, make tougher first offers, press harder for concessions, and resist conceding more than they would if they were negotiating with men.

Story after story, experience after experience provides compounding testimony that in today's reality, a large part of the wage discrepancy of professional women getting only 75 percent of the compensation that their male counterparts with similar experience and education receive is arguably attributable to these two phenomena, locus of control and the societal-cultural syndrome.

So what?

The net of all this is women don't ask. They don't ask for a whole complicated set of reasons, but that is precisely the point of the aforementioned books and this book too. It doesn't hurt to ask. If you choose to engage in requestive channel negotiation, let me reiterate my three promises: If there is more to get, you will get at least some of it, maybe all of it. You will never put your offer in jeopardy by engaging in RCN, and even if you get nothing, which occasionally happens, you will have the peace of mind of knowing that no one (and certainly no man) could have negotiated a better offer for that job at that point in time. You will have *maximized* your offer, and the pot of honey will be building in your bank account, not your employer's.

CHAPTER

15

Testing the Final Offer, Poking the Bear, and Getting Perilously Close to Ultimatum Channel—for Advanced Users Only

I'm going to throw an effective but seldom used technique that is worthy of your consideration, but be careful with its use. As you already know, at the final stage of obtaining your new job, there are four channels: ultimatum, demand, requestive, and probative. The first three are legitimate channels of negotiation. The last, probative, is not a negotiation channel; it is simply a communication channel used to achieve clarity about all things related to your employment offer. Probative inquiry is utilized throughout the employment process from the first phone call all the way up to your offer stage. You need to have the answers to all your questions before you start negotiations. Probative channel, like RCN, also has a question mark at the end of the sentence, but it is not used to gain anything other than clarity and understanding. Examples are: When do the major medical benefits start? How is success measured in this culture? Is membership in professional associations encouraged? How's the cafeteria food? These are examples of probative inquiry designed to get you information that you might use in your negotiations, but there are only three legitimate channels of negotiation according to the Milligan School of Industrial-Strength Salary Negotiations.

Ultimatum channel has its place and can be used to your advantage depending upon your circumstances. Remember the three conditions that must exist for negotiations to start: you have to be the successful candidate, the job has to have a range, and you must be emotionally committed and sincerely want to work for this employer (see chapter 5). While the first two conditions are always a must have, the third condition will vary according to your circumstances. Most always, the meter on condition number three is something less than compelling. When engaging in ultimatum channel, you have to remember most of the deals in this channel get left on the cutting room floor. The failure rate is over 50 percent.

Demand channel occupies a much more useful (and more successful) place in your toolbox, but it too has a measurable failure rate. While this channel is direct and efficient, remember that the organization always has alternatives (just like you do), and they may not be in a mood to acquiesce to your demands. Most notably, in the larger world of negotiations, when an offer is tendered, if it is met with a counteroffer (which is what a demand actually is), the original offer becomes null and void. That original offer is quite literally taken off the table at the moment a counter offer (demand) is presented. The employer at that moment is actually free to accept, reject, counter, or simply walk away, secure in the knowledge that there is no further obligation. The tables have turned. This not-so-subtle fact of life in negotiations is played out every day around the world. So demand channel too has risk and the possibility of failure.

Requestive channel is the only one of the three that has no risk of failure. It is the art of asking a question. What happens when you ask a question? You get an answer—maybe yes, maybe no, maybe something in the middle. But the other side does not fold its tent and leave the room. Like I've said, I have never personally experienced nor have I ever known of a single example of any employer rescinding an employment offer as a result of a candidate asking a question. What happens is that you get an answer, and frequently it leads to something tangible and something you can take to the bank.

In my experience, it leads to something tangible nine times out of ten. Occasionally you get a no answer. However, here is another sleeper benefit that comes to you from engaging in requestive channel negotiation. When you get a no, it comes with a full, complete, and almost apologetic explanation of why. Example: Let's pick up at the point where you asked, "Do you have any flexibility in the base cash compensation offer of $65,000?" The no response sounds like this: "Actually, we don't. The hiring manager and I pulled out all the stops to get the offer up to $65,000, which, you see, is the midpoint of our range, and we are pretty much forbidden to go above midpoint with new employees." You can rest assured that is a no answer, but it came with a full explanation as to why it is a no.

At this point, your offer is still intact, and you are presented with more alternatives about whether you want to negotiate for tomorrow (see chapter 16) or shift strategies to request something else as a quid pro quo, like a hiring bonus or an accelerated first review. Or you can accept the offer with peace of mind, knowing that you have just maximized your offer for this job at this point in time. Notably, your offer is intact; you haven't engaged in any acts of brinksmanship that might damage relationships or give the employer any occasion to withdraw.

If you are so inclined, there is one more remaining tactic you can try. It is still a requestive channel technique and allows you to explore the employer's commitment to closing the deal or their adherence to rules and policies. You can test the employer's full, complete, and almost apologetic explanation by going one step further, which, by the way, gets very close to using ultimatum channel technique. As in the above example where you just received the explanation as to why it is a no, you proceed with, "So what you are telling me is that you have no room to negotiate the $65,000 offer; it's a take-it-or-leave-it proposition. Is that it?"

Now, this is not for the faint of heart, and that is why I say it is for advanced users only. Technically you are still in RCN because there is a question mark at the end of your sentence. But what you have just done is put the employer in the position of issuing you an ultimatum, and I assure you no employer is comfortable with being in that position. When you do this, you test the bounds of the offer, and you put the employer in an awkward position, but you are still technically in RCN, and you will get an answer. It may be, "Well, perhaps I should revisit with the hiring manager (or other decision makers) and see what we can do," which is not a yes but is not a no either. I have worked with some truly exceptional candidates who seized the moment to conjure up a gold-plated sentence like, "Thank you. As you speak to them, please reflect on the amount of experience I have in the industry, the competitive knowledge I bring to the table, and the value I can add by being able to hit the ground running ... so to speak. These might be good reasons for going above the midpoint."

Sounds incredibly high risk, doesn't it? But this technique is still in RCN, and you will get an answer. It may be "no," but even then, you will get an explanation, and your offer will be intact. Most likely they will realize that rules are made to have exceptions occasionally, and they will offer a bit more, for which you will express profound appreciation. Then you will turn the discussion to asking the next question, "When can I start?"

CHAPTER 16

Negotiating for Tomorrow

One of the available alternatives to poking the bear and testing the final offer is the comparatively low-octane option of negotiating for tomorrow. This is a simple stutter step in the process of negotiations that we need to keep in our mental checklist as we count down the employment process to "I accept" and "When can I start?"

If it appears that we are all done negotiating for today, before we wrap up the negotiations, we should consider negotiating for tomorrow. I like to call this step the true test for maximizing your offer. It represents a last-ditch effort to obtain something tangible from the negotiation process when it seems that all we have gotten is "no." Likewise, it represents an alternative to just accepting the full, complete, and almost apologetic explanation why you received a no to your perfectly formed requestive channel negotiation question, "Do you have any wiggle room in that offer?" It goes like this: "Well then, thank you for that explanation. I understand completely, and my enthusiasm for joining Acme Tool Company is not diminished at all. But tell me, if I were to come on board at your current offer and demonstrate my ability to add value in a real and credible way, would you entertain a salary and performance review in six months rather than a year?"

This is what I call asking them for the sleeves out of their vest. It is an important if hollow victory, and any time you don't want the extra cash created by getting the first review in six months, just send it to the Jack W. Milligan retirement fund, and I will make good and proper use of it.

Also under this category is the often-overlooked reality that you may not be eligible for any time off with pay for a full year. If you have pending and identifiable life commitments on your time horizon, this is the time to bring them up and request (RCN) some time off (with pay) to attend your daughter's graduation or your mother's induction into the Daughters of the American Revolution or your son's release from juvenile detention. At this point in the negotiations, the company might be looking for things to say yes to. Sometimes, asking for an accelerated review after you come on board and demonstrate your abilities can get you an economic review in six months rather than waiting a full year. But it won't happen unless you ask for it.

Lastly, under the category of negotiating for tomorrow is the notion of severance or termination pay. Remember that all jobs are temp jobs, and I guarantee you that your bright, shiny, new Maserati of a job will fade to nothing at some point in the future (see silver bullet story, chapter 17). All jobs end. Some end happily, and some end with much drama. Some just end. Ultimately, they all do.

At the time of this writing, there is no federal law that compels an employer to give severance pay. Many companies do have severance policies, and among those that do, the most popular formula is one week of severance pay for each completed year of service. The determination of a "cheap" or a "rich" severance policy when measured by that standard can vary a bit, but no such formula-based severance plan will do you much good when you have little service with the company. That is why you might want to include an item like severance or termination pay in your negotiating items short list (NISL, see chapter 5). Should you lose your job through no fault of your own, the notion of having an economic cushion (severance) to protect you and your family lifestyle is not an unreasonable request.

Compared to the rest of the developed countries in the world, the USA is still the Wild West, where the doctrine of *employment at will* means that in the absence of a contract, your employment can be terminated at any time, with or without notice, with or without cause. At-will employment in the global sense is the least restrictive and least costly employment relationship to terminate. At-will employment in America has been seriously eroded over the past fifty years by various social legislation, court decisions, and aggressive administrative interpretation, but the doctrine is alive and well. Trust me, you will be well served if you accept the knowledge that this job shall end, before you even start. That realization will make it a little easier for you to negotiate for that inevitability.

The accepted thinking is that the higher you go in the employment hierarchy, the longer it will take you to find something comparable. One of the ways to hedge your bets is to negotiate severance into your offer package. As economic conditions change, so does the required job-search time. Obtaining three to six months of a financial cushion will help immensely and softens the economic strain on you and your family. Recognizing that we live in the global equivalent of the Wild West, it would be financially prudent to make certain that you have these contingencies covered. Work hard and be prudent with your finances and make certain that you have sufficient reserves to take care of your needs in uncertain times.

Over my years in career counseling, I have worked with the full spectrum of readiness for hard times that come, and I strongly suggest to you that your stress level will reduce, your anxiety will fall, and your life will be better if you prepare for financial hard times by having the necessary resources to see you through.

One way or the other, shifting this burden to the company in a preemployment agreement is good, but even that is not a guarantee. Companies go bankrupt all the time, and your offer letter entitling you to six months of severance does not amount to much of a claim if your company is in bankruptcy. Wage claims of this nature tend to go to the end of the line of creditors. Nevertheless, getting such an agreement is far preferable to not getting one. Your individual circumstances will dictate if this rises to the level to be included in your own NISL, and if it is, then all you have to do is ask!

All Jobs Are Temp Jobs— the Silver Bullet Story

Buried deep in the basement catacombs of every HR department is a secret room with a locked door. Very few people have the key to this door, and there is a blood oath among them to never discuss even the existence of this room—and certainly not its high-value contents. Were you to somehow gain access to this room, you would discover row upon row of bright, shiny, .45-caliber, silver bullets, all arranged very neatly and each one engraved with the name of an employee. Upon close examination, you would see empty spaces where once there was a bullet. And there they all sit, waiting.

As the legend goes, when you join the company, one or another of the secret key holders is commissioned to cast the next .999 pure silver bullet, polish it to a high luster, and engrave it with your name. Once properly loaded with the right amount of gun powder, the high-luster silver bullet is seated in the casing, and the polished projectile takes its place on the shelf in line with the others in a seemingly endless continuing serpentine of bright, shiny objects circling round and round the room perimeter. And there your bullet will sit, waiting.

The absence of cobwebs and other artifacts of neglect indicate that this deep, dark, and secret room is regularly attended to, but only legend speaks to the room and its shiny contents with intermittent voids in the otherwise continuous shiny silver line. And there they sit, waiting.

The only question, according to the legend, is how and when are you going to get your silver bullet? Will it be a neatly wrapped package with a big bow on top as a high-value token of your long service and given to you at your retirement party? Or will it be loaded into a .45-caliber handgun to dispatch with you? Figuratively speaking of course.

How you get your silver bullet depends on an infinite set of variables, but eventually, sooner or later, voluntarily or involuntarily, you get your bullet. Guaranteed. All jobs are temporary.

Your bullet is a reminder that all jobs are temp jobs. Sooner or later, you will leave this employment relationship. It is an absolute certainty—no maybes, no equivocation, and no kidding, all jobs end. Only the current employees still have their shiny silver bullets there on the shelf in that deep, dark, and secret place. All the other bullets, in one way or another, have been given back to their namesakes.

Most workaday folks don't spend much time thinking about the reality that all jobs come to an end. It is almost always an unpleasant reality, and not thinking about it is our way of avoiding this untidiness. It's human; it's natural not to think about it. However, faced with that reality, envisioning the end before you begin can be a strategic advantage. Knowing with certainty that this job will end someday allows you to embrace that reality in a nonemotional way. Beginning with the end in mind is one of Steven F. Covey's Seven Habits of Highly Successful People. This notion that in the grand scheme of things, this job, like all jobs, will end can be liberating.

Whenever you become so wrapped up in the stress of work issues, this thought alone might help bring you back to what is really important in life because, guess what, life ends too. Jobs are merely a means to an end, and far more important things are happening all around you outside of work. Your top three priorities in life, it seems to me, are yourself, your family, and your career, not always in that order. Sure, there are plenty of other priorities in your life and lots of things tugging at you for attention, but my bet is that those are your top three. Now, the priority may move around from time to time. Surely there are circumstances that require that your family comes first. Alternatively, your work may, from time to time, inundate you with (temporary) consuming priorities, and without a doubt you have to take care of "you" issues or not much else matters.

Work is important, clearly. Work is what allows you to do what you want with what remains of your time. Work, therefore, is a means to an end. Work is what you do, not what you are! You are expected to be much greater than your work, so keep your top three priorities in perspective and move back and forth among them to achieve the balance you need in order to maximize the returns on your work investment. I want you to maximize your total wealth. In order to do that, all you have to do is ask!

CHAPTER

18

Employment Agreements and Termination Agreements

While I have been clear throughout this book that I am not a researcher and this is not a book containing such scholarly and well-documented material that it is a candidate for journal publication, I would like to also let you know that neither am I an attorney. I do have a lot of experience working with attorneys, mostly employment and benefits attorneys. Inevitably, over many years, some of this legal stuff is likely to rub off. So some of the things I say in professional situations and teach in my HR classes might sound like legalese, but make no mistake, I am a fan of getting proper legal advice when you need it. This chapter on employment/termination agreements is very close to being over my pay grade. So let me warn you, this is not legal advice, and if you are in the strata where legal agreements are likely to be part of the deal, then please follow my advice and get proper counsel.

If you live in the United States or any of its territories, protectorates, or possessions, you live in a country where all jurisdictions, save one (Montana), observe the doctrine of employment at will. This uniquely American doctrine means that in the absence of a contract to the contrary, your employment can be terminated by both you and by your employer "at the will of either party" at any time, with or without notice, with or without cause ... so long as it's not for a "bad" reason. That last phrase has been added by legislative and common-law decisions over that past four to five decades and represents an erosion of the original doctrine. A "bad" reason is any illegal reason, such as making an employment decision on the basis of age, sex, race, religion, national origin, or any other legally protected category.

One of the best attorneys in the executive compensation business is Alisa Baker, who is a partner in the San Francisco law firm of Levine and Baker. Ms. Baker has also written two books on the source of real wealth creation for executives, which is variable compensation and, more specifically, equity (stock). She wrote *Selected Issues in Equity Compensation,* which is [#25] the layperson's guide to stock-based compensation. This subject has a lexicon all of its own, and Ms. Baker does a grand job of translating that language into plain talk we can all understand. She also authored *The Stock Options Book,* which is [#26] now in its eighteenth edition and is also used as a teaching text on the subject ... at Stanford. Ms. Baker knows her stuff, and if you ever need wise counsel or representation on any executive compensation subject, she or someone she refers you to will serve you well.

I spent almost two decades of my career with a publically traded, Fortune top-fifty, American-based, global conglomerate where less than 1 percent of US domestic employees were covered by a contract, whereas in Europe it was not uncommon for secretaries and administrative assistants to have contracts. Employment agreements and contracts are much more fashionable in other developed countries than in the USA.

There is no real line in the sand that you cross in your career that determines you now are entitled to a contract. Employment agreements (as they are also known) are rare in the United States as compared to other nations, primarily due to that old doctrine of at-will employment. At-will employment relationships cover most of the noncontract-based jobs and, for the most part, work quite well. Only time will tell whether Montana has gone totally rogue and off the reservation with their Wrongful Discharge from Employment Act (WDEA), which prohibits terminations except for good cause.

Or Montana might just be the very tip of the emerging iceberg for the Model Employment Termination Act (META), which has been floating around since 1991 when the Conference of Commissioners on Uniform State Laws recommended its enactment in all states. It is still out there and looking for traction. META is essentially similar to a "good cause" standard for termination. Like I said, only time will tell.

At any rate, should you be presented with an employment agreement, it generally means you have arrived at the supernova level where you need counsel. Don't try to fake it. Don't just sign it. Get counsel. Most of your agreement will probably be boiler plate and nonnegotiable, but it will also include issues related to noncompete and intellectual property and assorted other restrictions on your future. You might just reflect back on my last chapter about all jobs being temp jobs and then fast-forward to the inevitable date when you will be leaving the employ of this organization. You will be very glad that you sought counsel first and negotiated the narrowest restrictions possible on your future.

Switching the subject to termination agreements, they are a hundred thousand times more common (approximately) than employment agreements, and a termination agreement might just be as simple as drafting a few more sentences into your original employment offer. Reflect back to the anatomy of an offer (chapter 5). You used some of your magic time to consider your alternatives before calling the hiring manager back. One of the issues you might want to put on your negotiating items short list (NISL) is a termination agreement. You can also call it a severance agreement if you like. Just as enforceable as any agreement or contract, your offer letter stands as written proof of the terms and conditions under which you accepted employment and came on board. Please don't accept a verbal agreement from your hiring manager. Get it in writing, make certain a copy goes in your official file in HR, and for heaven's sake, keep a copy in a safe place.

Severance is a perfectly legitimate request to make as part of the bargain to leave your current employer. Even if you are unemployed you still have leverage. You just need to create a compelling argument for the company to provide extra financial protection against unforeseen circumstances. At the "ask" stage, it might sound something like this: "Joining Acme Tool Company is the career event of a lifetime for me and my family, and I'm very excited to get started. As you know, I have been with Intrepid Corporation for a number of years, and one of the important benefits I enjoy is their severance policy, which kicks in if I lose my job through no fault of my own or due to unforeseen business circumstances. Now, as I understand it, Acme has no severance policy, and this is an important security issue for me and my family. I am hopeful we can add a special understanding to my offer that will provide me an equivalent amount of financial protection should something unforeseen happen at Acme. I am not asking for Acme to underwrite my performance … only if something unforeseen happens and through no fault of mine I lose my job. Is that possible?" Remember to stay in requestive channel; this is an "ask." It certainly won't happen unless you ask, and chances are good if you exercise the patience and courage to phrase a compelling case, the employer will agree to write it into your offer. If you ask, and they say no, you are no worse off, and you might still consider negotiating for tomorrow (chapter 16), like maybe a signing bonus as a quid pro quo for the severance agreement. Either way, you still have the offer on the table. But you do have to ask.

CHAPTER
19

Settling into the New Job

Harvard Business School Professor Michael Watkins published *The First 90 Days* in 2003 [27]. In 2013, he put out a tenth-anniversary edition, brushing up some new material but staying true to his original. He and Dr. Dan Ciampa had published an earlier work in 1999 titled *Right from the Start*, which [28] left him knowing there was more to the notion of "accelerating the transition" that he still wanted to develop.

In it he presents a road map for taking charge in your first ninety days in a new management job. The first days in a new position are critical because small differences in your actions can have a huge impact on long-term results. This is a very good book, and if you are serious about settling into your new job successfully and sowing the seeds for future successful performance, I suggest you invest in it. As a matter of fact, at Leathers Milligan & Associates, we frequently presented a copy to candidates when they landed in order to help them mentally align for the new challenge. Invariably, those who actually read it called later to say what a difference it made and to thank us for providing it.

The First 90 Days will equip you with strategies and tools to get up to speed faster and achieve more. This summary will show you how to diagnose your situation and understand its challenges and opportunities. You'll also learn how to assess your own strengths and weaknesses, how to quickly establish priorities, and how to manage key relationships that will help you succeed.

So clearly I plan on borrowing heavily from Dr. Watkins's suggestions, but no summary here can substitute what you will gain by reading it thoroughly. Before the Watkins book was published, my colleagues in outplacement coaching and I would make a point of debriefing each and every successful job-finding candidate on the nature and content of their hundred-day plan. This actually prepared candidates pretty well for that initial period, which we in the career-coaching trade have known for some time is mission critical to success down the line. This process became easier when we started just gifting graduating candidates with a copy of the book.

We did learn, however, many of the books ended up on home library shelves rather than yielding the preparatory benefit that we intended. So we returned to an interactive session, using the Watkins book as a guide. With this, we got the mental alignment, the sense of urgency, and the focus on early victories that we desired from our candidate. Most of them sincerely appreciated this session. This was the start of a business model that actually became part of our on-boarding services later on.

There are three stages to almost any person's search for a new job. The first (intake) stage has to cover a lot of ground because many people are not mentally and emotionally prepared to make a quick trip down the road to finding the new job. Most have to work through issues having to do with the job just departed. That notion figures into Watkins's process as well, and working through those issues is critically important. Learnings (and emotions) must be properly catalogued, and that takes time. It is imperative that those old issues be properly compartmentalized, as carrying them into the new job can be immediately toxic.

The second stage after coming to grips with the emotional and physical reality of your situation is what I call the "get ready," which includes the preparation of all your marketing documentation, and the third and final stage is the conduct of your search. All of which is behind you now as you start settling into the new job phase. But the importance of having a plan for your search has just been replaced with having a plan for your successful integration to the new challenge.

I want to remind people, whether or not they read the Watkins book, that the integration and on-boarding experience at the new job resembles a crash course in learning a new language. One must be totally immersed in the new environment, sensitive to the vertical learning curve before them, jettison the old baggage, reach out and develop new alliances, and osmose the culture and the business strategy equally as new and compelling learning assignments. One must embrace a new set of friends, colleagues, and teammates, all the while finding ways to enjoy new victories as they occur. Accepting the new challenge mind-set and enthusiastically embracing new learnings opens us up for marvelous new experiences. Getting out of the old comfort zone of hardwired, preconceived notions about solving problems (no one likes a know-it-all, particularly a new know-it-all) so they can more easily adopt new mental models is an important transitional experience. For almost the entirety of the first ninety days, the ask is so much more appropriate than the tell.

You must really get out of your office, manage by walking around, and learn the new business first from the core responsibility that you have been hired to fulfill. Next, to understand the upstream and the downstream implications of what you were hired to do, you need to open up a dialogue with your fellow colleagues in both those areas by engaging in positive inquiry about how you can complement and add value to what they do. Clearly, as soon as possible, you need to understand the strengths, weaknesses, opportunities, and threats (SWOT) that reflect the environment inside and surrounding your new organization. A thorough study of the organization's strategic plan is usually a good place to start.

The next challenge may take you much longer than the first ninety to one hundred days. Your industry and your new company's position within that industry will likely take you some time to fully understand. For you to feel comfortable with your ability to add value to your new organization, you must understand the entire business and economic environment in which the company exists. This is not to say you cannot make significant contributions almost immediately, but you must initially approach your integration much more like a sponge than like an oracle. Soaking up the learnings in your new company will be a critical first step. Whom you integrate with and how you go about it during this critical starting period will determine much of your future success. Pay close attention to the ways you want to influence this new environment and seek a mentor immediately.

Hundred-day plans, even if your new boss doesn't ask you for one, can be immensely valuable and will professionalize your entry to most any new environment. Having a plan makes the difference between success and failure, many times for no other reason than you thought it through. One of the very best templates you can apply to this tactical plan (which has strategic implications) is the ADDIE model: assessment, design, develop, implement, and evaluate. This closed-loop system constantly refreshes itself and leads to constant improvement (kaizen).

Please remember this over everything else during your first ninety to one hundred days: the ask is much more important than the tell.

CHAPTER 20

Free Agency—You Must Take Responsibility for Your Employability

It has been a long time since Curt Flood of the St. Louis Cardinals was successful in becoming the first Major League Baseball player to win free agency. Actually, it was Andy Messersmith and Dave McNally who were the first to benefit from arbitrator Peter Seitz's decision effectively nullifying the reserve clause in Major League Baseball that gave us free agency, but Curt Flood gets most of the credit because he took his case all the way to the US Supreme Court, and free agency became forever attached to his name, even though he lost the case. Since then, free agency has entered the lexicon of America and translates to being on your own and responsible for your own outcome. And so it is today—you are a free agent in the American labor force, and you must take care of you.

Nothing is so certain in this world as change. As things change around us, we must change as well, lest we be left behind. Your commitment to yourself is the most important one in life. Taking care of yourself is job one. Keeping your saw sharp means preserving and enhancing the greatest asset you have—you and your skill set. It is a concept of universal importance that was created and made popular in *The Seven Habits of Highly Effective People* by Steven

(#29) Covey. It means having a balanced program for self-renewal in the major areas of your life. Initially, Covey articulated four of these areas. I adopted the expansion to five major areas after a talk by Dr. Jim Tunney, whom you may remember as the dean of NFL referees, who made an indelible impression on me about goal setting in the personal, professional, family, financial, and spiritual sectors of our lives. Dr. Tunney reinforced something that intuitively resonates within me.

People who set goals tend to accomplish more. Setting goals is what gets you focused out there on the horizon, so if you want to get out ahead of this change thing, start by setting specific, measurable, attainable, realistic, and time-based (SMART) goals. Write them down. When you accomplish one, scratch it off and set another one. Setting goals gives you the opportunity to make alternative decisions about how you are going to spend your most valuable commodity ... time. When you start choosing how to spend your time, it is an important step toward being in control of your life.

Taking control of your career also implies that you keep up with the currency of your chosen profession. A while back, many organizations used to work with their employees to identify and develop the skills necessary for upward mobility. Unions played a part, companies played a part, and the educational system pre and post high school, tech school, and college played integral parts in this continuous lifelong development of skills and competencies. Somewhere along the line, it became the employee's responsibility to keep their skills marketable.

Personal accountability is not a trait that people are born with. It needs to be learned. Management consultant Todd Herman defined personal accountability as "being willing to answer for the outcomes resulting from your choices, behaviors, and actions." Continuous lifelong education is very much with us; nothing is more passé than a twenty-year-old high school diploma or even college degree. Advancements in most fields require that employees engaged in those fields keep their skills up, and most have to do it themselves. It is really nice when the company foots the bill, but ultimately every person in the job market must take responsibility for remaining employable in their chosen field of work throughout their working lifetime.

There are several ways you can use your current job to advance your development. Again, you have to ask. Be proactive and brainstorm some ideas with your boss to get things going. Ask your boss to work with you to set up stretch goals that will take you out of your comfort zone and challenge you to try something new or different and acquire new skills and experience. Suggest taking a "temp role" where you job shadow or assume some or all of the duties of another employee. Volunteer to join a cross-functional team that provides you with new experiences and greater visibility in your organization. Jump in and make a request for a special assignment that exposes you to a different part of the company or even a customer liaison position. Do some research on a new trend in your field and give a presentation to your team or department on your findings.

Ask for feedback, getting the truth can be one of the most effective ways for you to develop skills you may be overlooking, and if you don't ask for feedback, your coworkers frequently won't provide it—same with your supervisor too. Feedback, given and accepted freely, improves your performance and demonstrates added value and development. Take to heart the feedback you've been given. Use it to identify areas for development and then follow through with appropriate and targeted action.

Make it a point to talk to your boss on an ongoing basis and be clear about your career goals—not just at performance review time. Letting your boss know what your aspirations are will make it a natural for you to ask for consideration when other upwardly mobile jobs open up. Keep the dialog going and continue to share your aspirations. If there is a particular role or career path you're interested in, talk to someone in that career path. Find out what KSAs (knowledge, skills, and abilities) you need to be successful in that role. Inquire about the entry paths into that work. Communicate your goals and your willingness to sacrifice to get promotional opportunities. Remember—you have to take control of your upward mobility. You won't necessarily know about the opportunities and resources available to you if you don't speak up.

This is not likely to change as the speed of technology continues to accelerate. As we look into the crystal ball to predict the careers of the future, current thinking is that generations to come will engage in multiple careers and may find themselves changing careers multiple times by completely retraining for a whole new career in midlife. Come to think of it, lifelong learning is happening right now. Lifelong learning has been required in the various professions for decades. The medical, legal, and accounting, even HR, fields require continuing education with specific renewal requirements.

So keeping your saw sharp is no one's responsibility but yours. The alternative means your KSAs will no longer be relevant, and when that happens, your employment alternatives narrow and perhaps evaporate. So please commit to lifelong learning, commit to keeping your saw sharp, and commit to setting goals. Oh, yes ... don't forget to ask.

ABOUT THE AUTHOR

In an effort to be open and transparent with my readers it is appropriate to let them in on my background and experience because it is that history that forms the bulk of my observations upon which this book is based. I am an HR guy. Never wanted to be anything else professionally, that is after I got the Army out of my blood. That part did not take long. Two years actually. Two years of full time duty in Uncle Sam's Army cured me of the romantic notions I had put away growing up as the eldest son of a career Army officer. After attending the United States Military Academy Preparatory School as an active duty soldier and still not making it to the Point (West Point) my heart was heavy.

At this point in my life, nothing outside the Army had occurred to me. I was very much a product of the environment in which I had been raised. My primary influences were provided by a very traditional family environment where the Dad worked and the Mom stayed at home to care for the children. To me traditional meant moving every year or two ultimately to all parts of the world including Japan, Okinawa and high school in Europe in addition to many duty stations all around the USA. It wasn't until my senior year in High School in Akron, Ohio where I had the good fortune of a temporary living arrangement with my paternal Grandparents that I realized my idea of "traditional" was actually a very narrow slice of growing up experiences. Everyone did not move every year and in fact, many of those "civilians" actually lived their lives in one place, with life long friends and extended families and one high school. Unlike my life which had taken me to five high schools in four years. Suddenly, traditional took on a whole new meaning for me.

The die was cast, however, and the wheels of my wanderlust had been set in motion by my early development and within two weeks of high school graduation, I enlisted in the Army.

It was precisely that life as an enlisted man that awakened in me that inherent curiosity that led me to a career in HR. Frankly, I was captivated by the differences among people, what made them tick, why they behaved in so many different ways under seemingly identical circumstances.

In the mid-sixties with my Signal Corps unit (the 586th Signal Company out of Fort Irwin, California) building up to be among the first to "gyroscope" to Vietnam it was precisely the variation in human behavior that focused my interest on why people behave in the ways that they do. I seemed to be drawn into the study of human behavior at work and once back in college I naturally gravitated to the study of people and work, individual differences, human motivation, reward theory and organizational dynamics. That interest in the basic questions about human behavior (including self interest areas like salary negotiations) would propel my career for the next forty years. The entirety of that career was spent in Human Resources.

After the service I attended Kent State University and tried to focus on engineering but my second Strength of Materials course slammed the door on engineering for me. I then focused on business, labor economics and industrial relations courses. I owe a debt of gratitude to Uncle Sam for having the foresight to create the GI Bill, for without it, my time in college would have been a real struggle financially. It was from the KSU campus that I landed my first job in HR (it was Personnel in those days). I went to work for Firestone Tire and Rubber Company in Ravenna, Ohio. My primary tutor, whom I still remember fondly and well was Don Ramsey. Mr. Ramsey was the Director, the chief supreme and high potentate, the commander in chief of personnel stuff. He was an "old soldier" for Firestone and the veteran of many far flung duty assignments.

Don Ramsey actually hired me even before my graduation, into the staffing department where I was assigned to an even greater mentor Norm Claus. Norm was one of those bosses that only the fortunate few get the developmental privilege to work for. Norm and I got along famously from the start, the chemistry was good, he was like a surrogate father in many ways. Norm was retired military himself having spent a career as a noncommissioned officer in the Air Force. He spoke with a slight stutter which belied an exceedingly agile mind and he taught me much about the employment world.

This job gave me my first introduction to high volume hiring: a hundred people a week. We actually worked at the Ravenna Arsenal. Firestone had the government contract to manage the Ravenna Arsenal and re-activating the place from mothball status it had enjoyed since the Korean War. We needed lots of people to put the Arsenal back on line and it was my job, in part, to staff it up. At least that's my recollection, and I'm sticking to it. Actually, I was a very small part of Norm's team of interviewing and staffing people who worked together to bring Ravenna Arsenal from 150 FTE's to around 5,000 employees at full strength. Norm also gave me an introduction to the fascinating world of labor relations.

In one of my fondest recollections of my early Firestone career, Don Ramsey, the grand poohbah of all things personnel, coming to my desk and asking if I wanted to get involved in Labor Relations. In the nanosecond of contemplation that it took me to consider this opportunity, I discovered my lips had already voiced the affirmative response my mind had just confirmed. My job, as it turned out was to be the "scribe". As an introductory job in labor, this is a good one. You get to sit at the table, you take the notes, you dutifully scribe all that is said by all parties, and you keep your mouth shut. If one is lucky, you get to speak during caucus but only to your own team and then only to report what someone else said. It is a truly wonderful learning experience, a humiliating one but wonderful nevertheless.

While at the Arsenal I was contacted about an opportunity to become the number two person (in a two person department) for Joy Manufacturing Company (now Joy Global) in beautiful New Philadelphia, Ohio. For those of you unfamiliar with the drop dead gorgeous countryside of rural Ohio, if you draw a line straight south from Cleveland, through Akron and on through Canton, in another 30 or so miles you get to the twin towns of Dover & New Philadelphia on the banks of the Tuscarawas River. It was my brief exposure to the field of labor relations that caught the attention of Mr. Don Crean, Personnel Manager for Joy Manufacturing Co. You see, Firestone had five unions at the Arsenal and every day of the week, it seemed, we were in a third step or fourth step grievance meeting, an arbitration, a hearing or a negotiations session with some one or other of these unions.

Don Crean, the epitome of clean cut, Ivy League educated, upwardly mobile personnel guys, had attended The New York School of Labor and Industrial Relations at Cornell. He was a major influence on my career and gave me numerous opportunities to learn, grow and make mistakes. It was Don that hired me into the Labor Relations Supervisor and Staffing Manager job at Joy. It was Don who proposed me to be a member of the team at Joy Manufacturing Headquarters (Pittsburgh) that would go unit to unit within Joy implementing the Hay Plan job evaluation project. As a teacher, trainer, mentor they didn't come any better than Don Crean. Don tutored me in the staffing and the labor relations work and under his guidance I learned a great deal. Enough, in fact, to be selected for the Hay Plan implementation team. Thank you Don.

It was as a member of this team that I got my a first hand look at a number of operations within Joy as I trained their management teams to design, analyze, create, evaluate and implement the Hay Salary Administration Plan throughout the Joy organization.

One of these projects in California, introduced me to the Joy Aerospace Products division and Task Corporation a wholly owned subsidiary. Not long after project completion and getting to know the management team, the United Automobile Workers Union came knocking on their door in an attempt to organize the production and maintenance workers. Because of my Hay Plan familiarity with the facility, and the management, my background in labor relations and because they had grown to the size where they needed a full time professional in place, they offered me the opportunity to mount the campaign and win back the hearts and minds of the people in the proposed bargaining unit. I jumped at the chance, I also lost the election. My first and only loss in a career that would include 9 union elections with a record of 8:1 overall.

Despite a vigorous campaign against the union, the UAW won the election, they were certified by the NLRB and we were invited to enter negotiations with the UAW. Even though I had lost the election, the management offered me the position as Manager of Employee and Industrial Relations and my wife and I moved from beautiful rural Ohio to Anaheim, California, we began contract negotiations and I was suddenly in charge of my first number one HR job at a 300 employee facility. Since I was the first full time HR person at this company, I was carving out new territory, but was responsible for a full range of typical HR functions including Labor Relations with the UAW, Staffing, Employee Relations, Compensation and Benefits, Health, Safety and Security, and Employee Development. As I reflect upon it now, I had no idea what I was doing and I needed a great deal more development time to be ready for the assignment I already had.

In the strange juxtaposition that the practice of labor relations pits its occupants, the relationships forged between HR professionals and their union labor counterparts are a mixture of bi-polar forces. It is possible to develop a significant respect even liking for the opposition in the practice the opposing forces of labor relations. Just such a relationship existed between me and the organizer to whom I lost the election, a wily negotiator by the name of Bruce Lee. Last time I checked, Bruce was still active in the UAW and occupied a lofty position in its hierarchy. Sometimes a bond of mutual respect exists between opposite poles of interest in the labor relations game. It was Bruce Lee (never underestimate the power of a good union rep) who suggested my name to Jim Turner, Vice President of Personnel and Industrial Relations for ITT Gilfillan in Van Nuys, California. Jim soon became my boss and started me on a twenty year career with ITT.

While we have not spoken in years, I will be forever grateful to Bruce Lee for giving my name to Jim. Jim Turner was a highly colorful character and both blessed and cursed with an ability to recall information with uncanny precision. Jim knew, names, places, faces, dates, trivia, fascinating facts and tidbits of information and he could recall all of this and more at will. He was a truly unique human being. He also had an intense dislike for our CFO and as legend has it, laid a black eye on this CFO while in discussions of some incendiary nature in front of our Chief Executive Officer. Thus came a premature end to the ITT career of Jim Turner within a year of the time I had met him.

Before his pugilistic engagement brought an end of his ITT career, Jim had the good judgment to hire me as the Labor Relations Manager for ITT Gilfillan. Our interview consisted of a flight in his personal aircraft, an ancient Mooney that he kept at the Van Nuys airport. Our flight was a relatively short one consisting of a jaunt up the California coast to Oxnard where we had lunch at a 94th Aero squadron Restaurant situated strategically at the end of the runway. During our short but crucial time together, Jim switched from interviewer to recruiter. Seemingly satisfied that I had the background to do the job, he switched to recruiting me into the ITT family of companies as a career move. He correctly sensed that I was looking at the Labor job at Gilfillan as a small step backward in my career. After all, at the ripe old age of 29 I had the top HR job at now 500 person facility where I was responsible for everything under the HR umbrella. Getting back into a Labor job was not my idea of career progress.

Truth was, Gilfillan was a much larger facility and the UAW bargaining unit alone was larger than my whole plant at Joy. Furthermore, I was dangerously close to getting fired from Joy for mis-judging a serious situation and I needed a new opportunity. Jim made a convincing argument about an ITT career opportunity not just a job opportunity.

I did well at Gilfillan primarily because of Bill Barrett who transferred in to replace the colorful Jim Turner. Bill Barrett turned out to be THE most significant influence on my personal and professional development, every professional deserves to have a Bill Barrett in their life and career. Gilfillan helped me obtain my BS degree in Management and Labor Economics at Cal State Northridge which led to a promotion back to a plant level HR position three years later at a ITT Semiconductor plant in West Palm Beach, Florida. Less than two years after that another promotion to HR Director of US Division of Semiconductors in the Boston area and two years after that we were back to California into the Director of Human Resources position at ITT's largest domestic manufacturing facility: ITT Cannon in Santa Ana, California.

One and a half years later another promotional opportunity, this time as Vice President of Human Resources at ITT Courier in Tempe, Arizona. Courier was in the business of computer peripherals and employed over 3,000 employees throughout the world. I stayed at ITT Courier facility for the next nine years. I completed my master's degree in HR and Organizational Behavior in night school and obtained my SPHR Certification through The HR Certification Institute. This was the first time in my whole life that my nomadic moving history stood still. I never got tired of going to work at Courier, I was blessed with a staff of HR professionals who were truly extraordinary and we did some remarkable and creative initiatives on the Human side of the enterprise.

One of those remarkable things was to move most of our manufacturing to the Pacific Rim and over the course of eighteen months, we downsized the organization by over 600 employees mostly in manufacturing. The management of that downsizing was a huge success, we placed all the employees who were downsized and not only did this project reap excellent press for our treatment of employees, it got me nominated for ITT's highest internal award, the Harold S. Geneen Award.

I did not win, but it was a thrill just being nominated. This same experience drew me very close to the outplacement industry for it was the outplacement process that we went through for our employees that deserved all the credit that I received in that nomination. It was through that huge and painful change initiative that I became truly aware that the value of a HR program is not what happens for the employees when times are good, but rather what happens for the employees when times are bad. The affinity I developed for the outplacement trade would reenter my life in a big way within just a few more years.

I thoroughly enjoyed my career with ITT and as mentioned above I retain a debt of gratitude to the guy who out maneuvered me in my first union election, Bruce Lee, and to the colorful Jim Turner who took me flying and sold me on a career not just a job.

The end to my ITT career came with the sale of the Courier division to private interests. It hurt me greatly to turn the Courier organization over to the new owners. I choose not to call them managers for management implies one knows something about getting things done through people. In private circles I gave the nickname of Attila the Hun to the new CEO in recognition of his insensitive and abusive management style. The saddest thing of all was that he liked it; he wore it like a badge of honor. When you can't find it within yourself to represent what your management team stands for, it is time to go, and so I did. After presiding over the transitional issues to the new firm, I took my leave from ITT after nearly 20 years and for the first time got a taste of a true job search. With the help of my new friends in the outplacement business I was able to land a new opportunity at the corporate level.

I had attained the level of VP of HR in a good-sized division of one of America's largest multi-national conglomerates but I had not attained my innermost goal of getting the top corporate HR seat. Working through Spencer Stuart (the headhunter firm) I accepted the position of Corporate Vice President of Human Resources for TransTechnology Corporation in beautiful downtown Sherman Oaks, California.

As it turned out, being on the 12 floor of a Los Angeles high rise building in terra-not-so-firma, convinced me that "fun" had somehow been squeegeed out of the job description in this company. I had accepted a top corporate HR job in a company that could not have been more wrong for me. I realize now, that I had been in pursuit of a goal that had lost its meaning long before I attained it. The most fun I ever had in my HR career was at the unit level where you have some control, some real influence, a budget where through the application of your wit, wisdom and intelligence you could make a difference in your employees' quality of work life.

I had known that the organization was planning to move to the East Coast at the time I was recruited. Our initial landing target had been Boston, the CEO's home town and first choice to relocate the corporate headquarters. It was fine with me and my family, having done a two year stint in Boston, courtesy of ITT Semiconductors, I was looking forward to returning.

Actually, anyplace where the earth did not move at the same speed as the freeway traffic would have been okay. But it was not in the cards, the military-industrial complex was cutting back on expenditures and we ended up co-locating our headquarters with one of our operating divisions in beautiful Newark, New Jersey.

Now, I have nothing against the fine Garden State but, as luck would have it, I did not make the team bus. Once again, I found myself in the midst of a career transition as I had been schooled to address it. Again, I contacted my friends in the outplacement business.

The rest, as they say is history. It is now twenty years later. The vast majority of that time I spent with a small boutique and independent outplacement firm in Phoenix, Murro Consulting. There I was able to learn the business through the help and assistance of the wonderful people who tend to gravitate to this extremely rewarding career field. Coincident with the new millennium I purchased an equity piece in the Phoenix based HR consulting firm and put my name on the door; Leathers Milligan and Associates. I was blessed with two superb partners, both of whom I had known for many years and suddenly I am totally immersed in the outplacement business, helping others through career transition.

Throughout my long and very rewarding career in Human Resources I have hired, been part of hiring, or taken credit for hiring over 20,000 people. Starting with Firestone where I personally hired fifty to hundred people a week to a Corporate vice presidency where we hired only a hundred people a month, I have been involved with making a few employment offers. Actually, hiring people is a really fun job. It is the happy side of the employment relationship. It is a place full of potential and promise and unfettered by all of the corporate politics that is sure to come.

Most of what you have read in this book comes from those years in the HR biz, but my thoughts and techniques did not start to jell into something to say about the employment process until I was involved in the outplacement business. I have worked with hundreds of people each year for the last two decades and each one helped me coalesce and formulate my techniques of Requestive Channel Negotiations. As I said at the beginning, I didn't invent any of this, I have simply put some labels on ordinary human behavior. Hopefully, these techniques will help you toward a slightly more comfortable life style. Please write me, send me an email, call me, and let me know your experience with these techniques. I wish you good negotiating!!!

jwm
JMilligan@LeathersMilligan.com

ENDNOTES

Chapter 1

1   Michael Watkins, *The First 90 Days,* 10th ed. (Harvard Business School Press, 2013).

Chapter 2

2   US Dept. of Labor, Bureau of Labor Statistics, www.DOL.gov.

Chapter 3

3   Roger Fisher and William L. Ury, *Getting to Yes, Negotiating Agreement Without Giving In* (Penguin Group, 1981).

4   Various authors of significance on the subject of negotiations: Stuart Diamond; Michael Wheeler; Alan McCarthy, Herb Cohen; all those at Dale Carnegie; Roger Fisher and William Ury and Bruce Patton; Deborah Kolb and Judith Williams; Linda Babcock and Sara Laschever—all worthy of reading.

5   Go to this site for an amazing math model of compound interest: http://www.thecalculatorsite.com/finance/calculators/compoundinterestcalculator.php

6   Linda Babcock and Sara Laschever, *Women Don't Ask: Negotiation and the Gender Divide* (Princeton University Press, 2003).

7   Linda Babcock and Sara Laschever, *Ask For It: How Women Can Use the Power of Negotiation to Get What They Really Want* (Bantam Books, 2008).

8   Jack Milligan, *Make More Money: The Fine Art of Asking—Most Don't* (iUniverse, 2016) (how self-serving).

Chapter 5

9   Sally Acree is not her real name.

10   Richard Woofter is not his real name.

Chapter 7
11 Roger Graham is not his real name.

Chapter 12
12 Bureau of Labor Statistics, Department of Labor, available at: WWW. DOL.gov.
13 Temporary Penetration Rate Reaches New High in August, blog post by Denise Martinez, September 17, 2014, available at http://www. jobscience.com/blog/temporary-penetration-rate-reaches-new- high-in-august/ and also at: https://www.oppenheimerfunds.com/ investors/article/temp-staffing-permanent-change-in-labor-force.
14 Peter Cappelli and Monika Hamori, *Who Says Yes When the Headhunter Calls? Understanding Executive Job Search*, 2014, research paper published by Wharton School, University of Pennsylvania. Sourced also at the International Association of Corporate Professional Recruiters.
15 $10.4 billion (source: the Association of Executive Search Consultants, 2011).

Chapter 13
16 Kanter and Streitfeld, "The Amazon Way," *New York Times*, August 15, 2015.
17 Ann Rhoades and Nancy Shepherdson, *Built on Values: Creating an Enviable Culture That Outperforms the Competition* (Jossey-Bass, 2011).
18 Jack Zenger and Joseph Folkman, *Harvard Business Report* article, 1/24/2013, Harvard Business Press.
19 Jack Zenger and Joseph Folkman, *The Extraordinary Leader: Turning Good Managers into Great Leaders* (McGraw-Hill, 2009).

Chapter 14
20 Babcock and Laschever, *Women Don't Ask* (2003).
21 Babcock and Laschever, *Ask for It* (2008).
22 Sheryl Sandberg, *Lean In: Women, Work and the Will to Lead* (Knopf- Doubleday, 2013)
23 Julian B. Rotter, "Internal versus External Control of Reinforcement," *American Psychologist*, April 1990.
24 Peter Smith, Shaun Dugan, Fons Trompenaars, "National Culture and the Values of Organizational Employees, a dimensional analysis across 43 nations," *Journal of Cross-Cultural Psychology*, March 1996.

Chapter 18
25 Alisa Baker, *Selected Issues in Equity Compensation*, 13th ed. (National Center for Employee Ownership—NCEO, 2013).
26 Alisa Baker, *The Stock Options Book*, 16th ed. (National Center for Employee Ownership—NCEO, 2015).

Chapter 19
27 Michael Watkins, *The First 90 Days*, 10th ed. (Harvard Business School Press, 2013).
28 Michael Watkins and Dan Ciampa, *Right from the Start*, (Harvard Business School Press, 2005).

Chapter 20
29 Steven F. Covey, *The Seven Habits of Highly Effective People*, (Free Press, 1989).

APPENDIX

Negotiable Items and Relocation Issues to Think About

Negotiable Items

- business-class or first-class travel
- country club membership
- hunting/fishing lodges and excursions
- limousine services
- concierge services
- educational sabbaticals, executive educational conferences
- spousal accompaniment on business trips
- use of executive aircraft
- financial advice and tax assistance
- legal advice and services
- executive coach
- automobile, maintenance and insurance
- executive physicals
- excess life and AD&D insurance
- health club membership
- personal trainer
- private use of corporate vacation resort
- attendance at corporate sponsored events (sports/political/ community, etc.)
- special long-term executive incentive plans
- stock grants, options, or equivalents
- golden parachute and/or handcuffs (retention agreements)

- executive severance agreements
- change of control guarantees

Relocation Issues

- house-hunting trip with spouse
- use of a relocation company
- temporary living expenses for ninety days minimum, depending upon personal needs, up to a year
- return trips home every two weeks and four-day week every other Friday and Monday extended family time
- full relocation of household goods, with insurance
- settling-in expenses of two months' compensation, with gross up
- all costs associated with purchase and sale in both from and to locations
- use of home purchase company in old location with 95 percent of equity offered immediately
- use of rental automobile in new location for reasonable period until personal vehicle can be transported
- tax preparation assistance at new location first year with CPA
- final gross up of all taxable items and gross up on the gross up
- special needs (if applicable)
- special needs of sandwich generation executives for caregivers—parents, children, extended family/friend relationships
- hobbies
- personal aircraft
- boats
- second homes
- volunteer commitments

Open Book Editions
A Berrett-Koehler Partner

Open Book Editions is a joint venture between Berrett-Koehler Publishers and Author Solutions, the market leader in self-publishing. There are many more aspiring authors who share Berrett-Koehler's mission than we can sustainably publish. To serve these authors, Open Book Editions offers a comprehensive self-publishing opportunity.

A Shared Mission

Open Book Editions welcomes authors who share the Berrett-Koehler mission—Creating a World That Works for All. We believe that to truly create a better world, action is needed at all levels—individual, organizational, and societal. At the individual level, our publications help people align their lives with their values and with their aspirations for a better world. At the organizational level, we promote progressive leadership and management practices, socially responsible approaches to business, and humane and effective organizations. At the societal level, we publish content that advances social and economic justice, shared prosperity, sustainability, and new solutions to national and global issues.

Open Book Editions represents a new way to further the BK mission and expand our community. We look forward to helping more authors challenge conventional thinking, introduce new ideas, and foster positive change.

For more information, see the Open Book Editions website:
http://www.iuniverse.com/Packages/OpenBookEditions.aspx

Join the BK Community! See exclusive author videos, join discussion groups, find out about upcoming events, read author blogs, and much more! http://bkcommunity.com/